Practical
GARDEN
DESIGN

Yvonne Rees

GW00696759

The Crowood Press

First published in 1993 by
The Crowood Press Ltd
Ramsbury, Marlborough
Wiltshire SN8 2HR

British Library Cataloguing-in-Publication Data

A catalogue record for this book is available from the British
Library.

ISBN 1 85223 624 8

Picture Credits

Line drawings by Claire Upsdale-Jones.
All photographs are by Sue Atkinson except for those on pages
1, 2/3, 20, 30 (top) and 32 (top right and bottom right) which
are by the author. Other photographs are reproduced by courtesy
of the following: Oak Leaf Conservatories, page 24 (bottom);
Briastone/R.S. Tripper, page 30 (bottom); Froyle Pottery, page
29 (top right) and Dobies Seeds, pages 19 and 63.

Typeset in Optima by Chippendale Type Ltd,
Otley, West Yorkshire
Printed and bound in Great Britain by
BPCC Paulton Books Ltd

CONTENTS

INTRODUCTION

We have all been envious of the kind of gardens seen or visited at national shows and festivals, or featured in books and on television. Whatever its size and theme, every square metre seems perfectly planned and exquisitely maintained. Yet you don't need the services of a professional landscape architect and an army of gardeners to transform your own humble plot, however small or unruly, into a similar private paradise, offering those plants and features you have often dreamed of. Nor does it require a limitless budget to create the garden or backyard of your dreams. A little imagination and attention to detail at the planning stages is more likely to create a successful and individual design.

If you can fix clearly in your mind the kind of garden you would like within the limits of the plot and resources available to you, it makes it much easier to choose individual features; while planning the design as a whole in the early stages pulls those features together and avoids any one item looking unnecessarily obtrusive or out of place. Drawing up a proper plan also provides the opportunity to control the look and feel of the final design.

You can make the plot look wider, shorter or simply more interesting for example, by choosing the shape and size of the major features carefully. Using plenty of curves in the design of paths, beds and borders disguises a dull square or rectangle. The position of paths and use of screens and trellis can add an air of mystery or divide the garden into more interesting, maybe more manageable, sections or 'garden rooms'. Certain features such as a statue, pool or lawn are naturally dominant and these act as a focal point, drawing the eye away from the garden's true boundaries.

If you give it just a little forethought, you can play tricks with shapes and colours, contrasting and co-ordinating just as you do with soft furnishings in the home. Some of the garden centres and flower catalogues are even offering co-ordinated collections and features these days. Or selective use of features and accessories might be used in combination to conjure up a certain theme or atmosphere such as a subtle oriental look or an unashamedly, brightly suburban garden. Planning your garden on paper certainly gives you something to aim at and helps immeasurably when it comes to buying individual elements; faced with a vast choice of styles, types and colours, you will know immediately which will suit your scheme best.

By all means use photographs and garden visits as inspiration: often an idea for a whole feature can be lifted and grafted on to your plan with just a few changes to add an air of individuality. Also, if the budget is a little tight, don't let lack of funds cramp your style. Consider using discarded or second-hand materials for your hard landscaping features. A lot of plants can be expensive, too, especially if you want to establish them quickly. Even seeds can work out costly if you only want a few plants of a certain type. So visit charity shops and bring and buy sales; arrange an exchange or share scheme between family and friends; or find out which gardens open to the public propagate and sell some of the more unusual plants. Propagating from your own existing stock of plants will provide extra material and give you something to barter with.

Another big plus to taking the time and trouble to plan your garden or backyard properly is that a well-planned design is easier to maintain, leaving you more time to sit back and enjoy it at your leisure. It's the way to make your garden work for you, whatever its size and style, rather than become an irritation and a burden. You will find lots of ideas and practical suggestions in this book – none of them too grand or difficult for even the smallest gardens Adapt them, scale them down or expand or them – the end result can only grow on you

1 • ASSESSING THE PLOT

A long, critical look at the canvas you have at your disposal is the first step before setting your heart on any features you might wish to imprint upon it. That canvas may not necessarily be a blank one, although the raw patch barely scattered with topsoil left by the builders behind most new homes can in many ways be more of a challenge than an established garden with a few mature features to be worked into the new scheme. Initially you should consider its size: it may be large and rambling, possibly even over-grown and defying you to make any sense of it. Here, dividing the plot into smaller, more interesting areas will make it easier to plan and to manage. Linked by paths and using screens and hedges as dividers, differ-ent areas could encompass a separate theme or feel; or be used for a variety of purposes – a seating area, for example, or a winter garden, offering maximum interest in the normally dormant months.

More often these days, though, the total size is painfully small to accommodate all the wonderful plans you have in mind. Again do not despair. Planning to scale will fit the maximum possible features into your pint pot without it looking cramped or overcrowded. Nor should you be fooled into thinking that scaling down features is the solution for small gardens and patios. Often a bold touch creates the impression of space and disguises the true boundaries of the area. There are many ways you can confuse the eye as to where the garden actually finishes: by dense planting, clever positioning of key focal points, a winding path. Strategically placed mirrors, *trompe l'oeil* effects and the use of water with its expanding, light-reflecting qualities, can all give the impression of extra space.

Shape

Shape can sometimes be a problem. You can turn an awkward shape to your advantage

The crab apple (*Malus*) genus includes a wide variety of deciduous shrubs and trees valued for their fine foliage, pretty spring blossom, autumn colour and glowing, edible fruits – indeed a garden-worthy plant. It prefers full sun but can be grown in shady spots and tolerates most soils. Spring flowers may be pink, white, red or purple and include both single and double forms – shown here is 'Montreal Beauty'; the fruits are yellow, red or purple tinged. Trees generally grow between 20ft (6m) and 30ft (10m) and there is a weeping version which is only around 12ft (4m) high so they are perfect for smaller gardens looking for plenty of interest through the year in the minimum of space.

by fitting in different features like a jigsaw puzzle. Some materials such as timber, particularly if you plan and construct them yourself, are better suited to made-to-measure features. More often though, you have a dull square or rectangle to contend with. This can be made to look more interesting by ignoring the basic framework beneath and planning a series of interlock-ing circles and other curved shapes, with a wandering path to avoid that sense of march-ing straight to one end and back again. Sometimes a plot will incorporate a signifi-cant slope or change of level; correction is always a tedious or expensive business, so try to accommodate it in your plans by steps or terracing or even by using the slope as a feature to build a waterfall, a rockery or alpine meadow effect.

Aspect

One of the secrets of successful garden design relies on choosing the right plants and features to suit their position. Conditions can vary considerably between one part of the garden and another, let alone regional and local differences depending on whether you live in the north or south of the country.

Vigorous evergreen climbers are always useful for providing all-year-round screening for privacy and shelter, especially when they have such large, glossy green foliage as *Rhoicissus rhomboidea*. This handsome tendril climber needs some support but will efficiently smother a wall, fence or trellis providing it is not in full sun and has a well-drained soil. *R. rhomboidea* will grow to a height of around 20ft (6m) making a dense curtain of deep glossy green leaves with bold veining. The plant should be well watered in hot weather and mulched at the roots to try to preserve moisture. It is frost tender but will tolerate temperatures as low as 7–10°C (45–50°F). Semi-ripe cuttings can be taken in summer or the plant grown from seed in spring. If the growth becomes too dense, stems can be thinned out in early spring.

Even a matter of miles can make a drastic difference between what can be grown in one garden and another. Prevailing winds, altitude, the extreme effects of something like the Gulf Stream or an exposed coastal location can all affect its general climate and determine whether you will experience below average temperatures, increased rainfall or subtropical temperatures.

Sited on the side of a hill, the effects of high winds will be more severe than on level ground; but valleys and other depressions receive sun later and do not benefit from warm air currents making them prone to being frost traps. Here they might remain covered with frost well into the morning when surrounding areas are clear. It makes sense to take note of what natural vegetation thrives in your area and observing what your neighbours are growing successfully in their gardens. Your own garden will have created its own microclimate, especially if it includes mature features such as trees, shrubs and walls.

It is a useful exercise to determine the general aspect of your garden before choosing your features; that is, in relation to the compass, which boundaries, as near as possible, face north, east, west or south. The north end of the garden will be south-facing and thus receive maximum light and sunshine. A wall placed here will act as a natural storage heater, absorbing radiant heat during the daytime and releasing extra warmth as the temperature drops at the end of the day. This is where you will want to position your more tender species of plants. The north-facing boundary of your garden will receive far less natural warmth and light and for plants to flourish here they must be the shade-loving species, the kind that generally grow in woodland or on the forest floor. You will also find that lighter coloured, sandy soils tend to be colder than richer, darker soils with plenty of humus as they retain less radiant heat from the sun. This makes them more susceptible to frosts

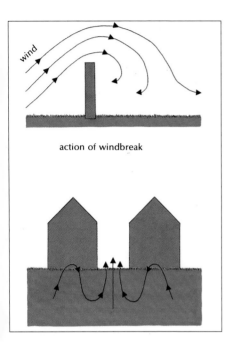

action of windbreak

(a)   A solid obstacle produces two sheltered areas: immediately before the windbreak and immediately after.
(b)   Two buildings close together can funnel wind through the gap creating a draught unsuitable for any plant growth unless a windbreak is created.

too. In addition, urban gardens are several degrees warmer than the norm, enjoying the heat and protection of surrounding buildings, traffic and local industry.

Observing your garden through the day will give some idea of the light and sun-shine levels; less easy to assess but equally essential to allow for is the wind chill factor. This is particularly important in exposed sites, in upland areas, on the coast or on roof gardens. Wind can kill or damage even established plants, and protection in the form of a windbreak will be required along the boundary facing the prevailing winds. A solid structure such as a wall or fence will

deflect the wind and provide shelter to plants immediately to the windward as well as the leeward side providing it does not exceed 3ft (1m). However, a broken screen such as a hedge is preferable in that some of the wind will pass through the gaps rather than travelling straight over the top of a solid obstacle, and thus dissipate the force of the wind instead of simply redirecting it. You should also beware of situations where the wind becomes tunnelled, say between two buildings, as very little will grow here without some kind of windbreak to alter the cruel draught.

Soil

It is equally important before going much further at the planning stages, to assess the type of soil your garden has to offer. As well as quite distinct preferences concerning sunshine and shade, many plants are quite fussy about the type of soil they require to thrive. The acid:alkali level of the soil is measured by a pH number from 1 to 14, the value 7 being neutral and equal to that of water. Most plants grow well between 5.5 and 8.5; some, for example azaleas and ericas, just cannot tolerate any alkalinity in the soil, others such as Potentilla and Iris which grow naturally on chalky ground, thrive on it. There are various soil-testing kits available which are simple to use; but it is important to test several areas of the garden, not just one, as results can vary quite considerably.

Soil type varies, too, from a heavy clay to quick-drying sandy soil. Clay soil is rich in plant nutrients but they are locked into the heavy material and need lime to release them. This is fine unless you are hoping to grow any lime-hating plants. The best way to improve a clay soil is to dig in plenty of humus, preferably before winter to give the frost a chance to help break it up and produce a fine tilth. Much lighter sandy soils are far more to the liking of acid-loving plants such as heathers and camellias. Thin and lacking significant humus-rich body and nutrients, they tend to dry out quickly and become impoverished. This will stunt the growth of most plants unless humus is added to improve both its nutrient levels and its heat-retaining properties. Leaf compost (using only the leaves from deciduous plants) is a useful and inexpensive mulch material for sandy soils. Gardens in downland areas sometimes experience chalky soil which tends to be well drained and quite good for growing vegetable crops but not suited to chalk-intolerant flowers and shrubs. The best kind of soil is loam which comprises small grains of sand (silica) with a large amount of body and nutrient-rich humus.

Soil in town gardens has sometimes turned what is called 'sour' – that is, spoiled from acid rains and pollution with very little goodness replaced from a continuous lack of proper gardening. It can sometimes be improved with the addition of lime to neutralize the acid at a rate of 20oz/sq yd (60g/sq m). The alternative is to remove the topsoil to a depth of about 24in (60cm) and replace it with good-quality loam; or to grow plants within the controlled conditions of containers.

Drainage

Drainage of your proposed garden must also be monitored if plants and features are to be successful. On a sloping site, water may drain away too quickly; on a level one, or in a depression, drainage may be so bad that the water table may rise above the surface. Sometimes a clay pan will stop the water running away, creating a permanently damp, water-logged soil. Not only will most plants die if the roots are constantly wet, the soil often becomes sour in winter. The answer is to lay an efficient

Bamboo is another architectural favourite for foliage groups, the tall elegant stems with their fluttering leaves like bright green prayer flags providing a wonderful contrast to other foliage types. They are related to other perennial grasses – this is *Arundinaria simba* – but have the familiar hollow woody stems which are extremely strong. Given the right conditions – a sheltered position and reasonably damp soil – most bamboos will become rather invasive and clumps need dividing regularly to prevent them taking over and smothering other plants. They can be grown in sun or shade and will do well in containers if the soil is kept well watered. They are perfect for adding an oriental atmosphere to a garden or patio scheme and can even be grown as a hedge or screen. Grown for their foliage, bamboos flower only infrequently and the flowers are not distinctive. After flowering the stems die back but the plant rarely dies altogether.

system of land drainage pipes to carry away excess moisture to a sump. If only a small area of the garden is poorly drained it may be worth considering a water feature such as a pool or a natural bog garden growing those plant species which prefer damp conditions (*see* Chapter 5).

Restrictions

Often the existing garden will include some permanent feature that is too costly or difficult to remove or which you would quite like to include in the new scheme. It is certainly useful to have a few mature features such as trees or an old mellow wall to make your new plans look more established. A little careful planning should ensure that these are attractively incorporated with other, newer features. An old tree might form a focal point for example, with seating built round the base. Or a pool be re-landscaped using other features to fit its surroundings more comfortably.

Sometimes that permanent feature isn't

Vinca minor var.

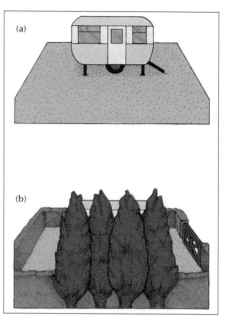

A parking area or outbuilding visible from the garden could spoil your plan.
(a)   Here a caravan on hardstanding needs hiding.
(b)   Trees and hedges have vastly improved the appearance of the area.

attractive at all and you would prefer it to be invisible. There are many ways an outbuilding, shed or even the coal bunker or rubbish-bin stand can be suitably disguised – behind a hedge, a screen or a trellis smothered in evergreen climbers. Should you wish to alter them or remove them altogether, take care that there are no legal restrictions governing existing features. Trees are often protected by a preservation order requiring permission to prune let alone fell them. You should always check with your local planning authority before felling or altering any tree. Some open-plan estates have restrictions concerning the style and height of boundary walls and fences so check these too before making any alterations.

2 • PLANNING THE MAIN FEATURES

Once you have made a detailed note of what you've *got*, you can concentrate on the kind of garden you'd like to *have*, then begin to work out how it might become a reality. There will be further limitations, of course: such as how much money you will have to spend on creating your new garden and putting those plans into action; how practical those plans might be – the gardens you find behind a town terrace often have limited access for machinery and large features, for example; and how much time you can spend doing it. If you can't do the work yourself, can you afford someone else to do it for you? Cost is going to be one of your biggest considerations. However, there are ways to economize, as mentioned in the previous chapter. The big advantage of working out a complete scheme for the garden in advance is that, given the opportunity to cost out your ideas before any real work starts, some features may be altered or even postponed, the garden being completed in stages. With an overall view of how the garden might look when it is finished, you should also have no problem buying the right elements at each stage.

Consider, too, before committing yourself to any particular features, how you would like your garden to perform. Is it to be a plantperson's paradise where you can spend many happy hours propagating and cultivating? A greenhouse, nursery beds and time-intensive herbaceous borders will

Front gardens are often neglected yet they create an important first impression and welcome visitors to the home. Here, paving the area makes it very easy to maintain and to clear up any rubbish that might blow in from the street, yet the use of old stone has kept an old-fashioned, informal feel. There is an evergreen backdrop for a small stone seat and a variety of plants in tubs and troughs.

be perfectly in order then. But if you have set your sights on an easy-to-maintain leisure area, you should be giving priority to the seating and barbecue areas and restricting plants to a strong background of evergreens with only a few seasonal interest plants demanding your attention. With careful choice of plants in raised beds and containers, a large water feature and automatic feeding and watering systems, your garden could be almost maintenance free.

How quickly do you want to see results? Long-term gardeners may be prepared to wait for trees to grow and perennial plants to mature. But if you are planning on moving home soon, an almost instant garden would be more appropriate, perhaps with loose-laid timber decking instead of paved areas and lots of bright, quick-growing annuals in containers to provide plant interest. If you have young children, your plans may have to be modified further with any pool areas well out of harm's way and suitable play surfaces or games equipment planned for. To work on a practical level, the garden must ultimately suit you and your family's lifestyle; while visually, individual features must fit together harmoniously to form an attractive whole.

Scoring with Boundaries

First define your boundaries and decide how they are going to be marked as this will affect the style of all your other features. Far from being dull, there is a wide range of choices, each well suited to a particular purpose and, unless your garden is very tiny, will represent a substantial outlay from your budget. It is a good idea to establish before you start exactly who is responsible for each boundary as the responsibility (and cost) may be shared with a neighbour. Fencing is easily erected and is good for privacy and shelter depending on the style you choose. It makes sense to buy good

Specially developed as a garden feature, the Japanese maples, *Acer palmatum*, are small, compact trees and shrubs renowned for their elegant foliage and brilliant autumn colouring. The popular variety *A. p.* 'Dissectum' is even more distinguished, growing no more than 5ft (1.5m) tall, making it suitable for bed, border or even a patio container if kept well fed and watered, and featuring leaves so finely divided they have a light, feathery appearance. *A. p.* 'Dissectum Atropurpureum' is particularly prized, spreading as wide as it is tall with a wonderful bronze-red, almost purple colour which turns a fiery red, yellow or orange in the autumn. For all its delicate appearance, the shrub is fully hardy but prefers a sunny position and a well-drained soil to show off the shivering foliage to best advantage. Small purplish flowers appear mid-spring.

quality as the cheaper types, such as interwoven larch panels, cannot withstand strong winds and once damaged become

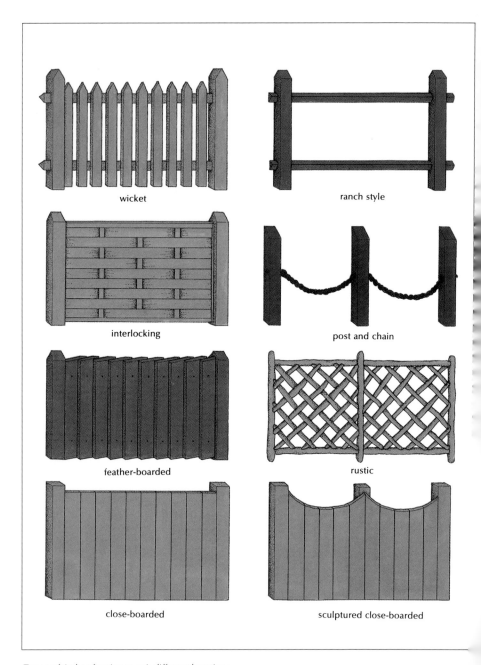

wicket

ranch style

interlocking

post and chain

feather-boarded

rustic

close-boarded

sculptured close-boarded

Types of timber fencing to suit different locations.

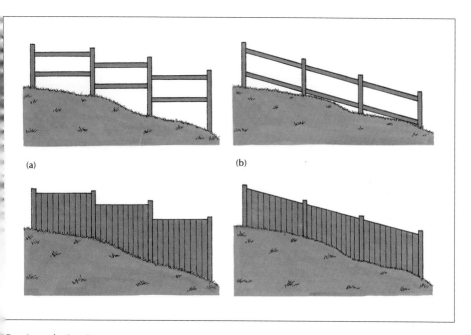

(a)

(b)

Fencing a sloping site.
(a)   Insert the main fencing posts 6ft (2m) apart, then screw the cross struts into position using a spirit level to get them straight. The fencing panels can then be fixed to the frame.
(b)   Where the fence follows the general slope of the ground, the highest and lowest posts are positioned first; then the depth to which the others are to be sunk is determined by stretching a piece of string from the top of one post to the other.

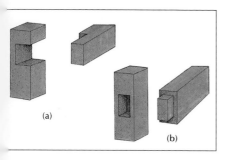

(a)

(b)

Fencing joints.
a)   An open joint suited to light structures in which the horizontal strut is much smaller than the upright.
b)   Where strong horizontal supports are used in the structure, a bayonet-type fitting should be used.

quite an eye-sore. The better-quality fences might be a simple country wicket, a rustic lattice effect or good solid close-boarded or feather-boarded fencing. Some of the close-boarded types are shaped in a decorative manner along the top. Other fencing styles such as ranch-style fencing or post and chain style are very open and really only delineate the boundary.

Walls are generally more expensive and a lot more time and trouble to erect. Dry-stone walling – that is building a wall without placing mortar between the stones – is quite an art and looks lovely in an informal or cottage-style garden. A more formal wall is built from bricks, stone or dressed slabs. The most popular types of stone for this purpose are Portland, Purbeck and Cotswold. Artificial and ornamental stones are also available but are used more for low patio walls or for building features around the garden. Importantly, any wall should be in keeping in colour and style with your house to make that link between home and garden more successfully.

Trellis is more likely to be used as a divider between different sections of the garden or to hide the shed or compost heap and is not strong enough to be erected as an external boundary. However, it is perfect for training climbing plants where you might wish to create a wonderful display of flowers and foliage. For a rustic look, the trellis may be constructed of larch poles; more substantial is second-hand planed wood for an instantly mellow look, nailed to an upright every 3ft (1m). There are companies producing highly decorative, solid timber trellis with ornamental gothic- and medieval-design posts and finials; this is naturally expensive but very stylish. They look so good it almost seems a shame to cover them in climbing plants.

Hedges take much longer to establish themselves but they involve no special skills and look highly attractive, being comple- tely natural. There is some maintenance involved, of course, as they will have to be trimmed back regularly during the growing season. Suitable shrubs are planted about 18in–3ft (½–1m) apart: the choice of plant material is almost limitless providing you trim any unwanted growth to shape as necessary. If you are looking for quick results, Lawson's Cypress is one of the fastest-growing evergreens and it can be trained to any height. By contrast, dark green yew grows slowly but is highly attrac- tive, but the berries are poisonous so this is not a practical option if you have children. A copper beech hedge remains popular providing a garden highlight of brilliant golden colour in winter; while for a more informal but dramatic look, *Rosa rugosa*

Berried shrubs and trees are useful for providing something of interest and a splash of colour in autumn and winter, but few produce such a prolific display as Cotoneaster. There are many different types, some of which can offer attractive foliage and flowers, too, and including ground-cover varieties. All prefer a dry soil which makes them useful for sites close to buildings. Evergreen types can be grown in semi-shade, but deciduous species prefer full sun. Each offers a range of different features be it good autumn colour, delightful flowers in spring, interesting fruits or attractive foliage, and they come in many forms from prostrate and arching types to bushy shrubs and upright trees.

can offer a dense hedge of beautifully scented flowers in summer, with a mass of bright rose-hips in the autumn.

Screens and Arches

While you are considering the right type of material for your garden boundaries, thi

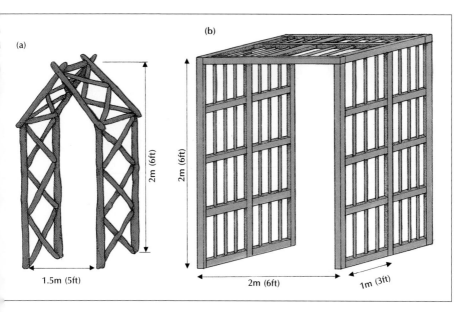

(a)

(b)

2m (6ft)

2m (6ft)

1.5m (5ft)

2m (6ft)

1m (3ft)

a) A rustic archway is simply constructed from larch or chestnut poles and can be used over the gate or within the garden scheme to support a climber rose or honeysuckle.
b) A pergola structure made from planed wood is a useful support for scented climbers with pendulous blooms such as Wisteria.

might be a good time to select any screens, partitions and archway or pergola structures. It is important that these vertical hard landscaping features are fully integrated into your scheme to look as natural as possible in relation to the rest of the garden. Screens and partitions are useful for hiding eye-sores or for dividing the garden into smaller areas. They might be made of trelliswork, mesh, or, for oriental style gardens, bamboo. Other means of adding height within the main garden scheme are decorative arches and walkways, often made from metal with a choice of patterns and designs; or if you prefer a rustic look, constructed from chestnut or larch poles. These might be used to create an 'entrance' to the main garden or simply lead to another part of it. Traditionally they are covered in flowering plants such as roses or wisteria.

One of the most exciting free-standing structures designed to display climbing plants such as wisteria, vines and clematis, is the pergola which takes the form of a covered area or pathway using an upright framework with battens across the top. A pergola looks equally good as a walkway (in which case it should be at least 6ft (2m) wide); or as an overhead shelter for a patio eating area, scented blooms dangling over the heads of the diners. The best-planned pergolas lead from one area to another, they never stand in isolation. You could use it to link two parts of the garden or to connect the main house to the garage.

Choosing the Features

With the main framework planned, you can

(a)

(b)

Enclosing a garden or leaving the plan essentially open creates a totally different look and feel.
(a)   has a far more informal feel yet remains easy to maintain thanks to large areas of attractive
paving instead of grass, and a mature arrangement of trees, shrubs and perennials as well as
annuals.
(b)   is more formal, ideally suited to a town garden. There is still scope for trees but they must
be restricted to 10ft (3m) and earn their keep by offering several features such as attractive
flowers, foliage, bark and autumn colour.

start choosing specific features. You will want at least one patio area (*see* page 25) positioned where it will catch maximum sunshine. Within that patio area you will have to decide on the facilities that would be most useful to you and your family or friends. Often such features can be built-in to the design in matching materials, whether that be stone, brick, timber or slabs; this not only looks good but maximizes available space, too. Your patio complex might incorporate seating with raised beds and maybe a formal pool. Often it is a good idea if you have the space to design more than one formal paved area within your total garden plan so that you can sit out at different times of the day. It is often useful to have a patio adjoining a summerhouse structure, surrounding a free-standing gazebo or helping to integrate a swimming-pool with other garden features.

If you have always fancied a water feature (*see* page 44 for details), now is the time to plan for one as any necessary excavation work will be easier and create less mess before other features are established. Remember that the site must preferably be a sunny one, away from any deciduous trees or shrubs that may foul up the water in autumn with their leaves. If you do not have room for some kind of pool, a smaller water feature such as a water spout or bubble fountain fits neatly into the smallest of corners in the garden or patio. A pool

A formal treatment often suits a sunken garden best and is a good way to deal with a natural dip or hollow that would be expensive to infill. Here the garden rises behind a large patio which adjoins the house, so co-ordinated bricks and paving materials have been used to create walls and raised planting beds. Strong shapes and colours among the plants is important to offset such a large area of hard landscaping.

can often be linked with other features: not just a waterfall or cascade joining two pools perhaps, but it could be combined with a rockery or flower-beds to blend it into the rest of the garden more smoothly.

Also consider now any other features you feel would be important: a play area for the children, a fine lawn, maybe a built-in barbecue or a hot tub or spa for those who do not have room for a swimming-pool.

Once the 'hard landscaping' is completed, features and any less attractive but essential garden areas such as sheds, greenhouses, composting area or rubbish bins, will have to be linked by a series of paths, bridges, stepping stones or walkways to provide easy and safe access particularly when the weather is wet. These are covered in more detail on page 32, but it is important that they are attractive as well as functional. Materials used must be in keeping with the rest of the garden and it is more interesting if they can follow a fairly circuitous route taking in other features rather than going directly from A to B.

Lighting

The final, yet very important touch for any successful garden design is the lighting. This feature should not be an afterthought, but, for best results, should be considered in the early stages of planning to achieve the right effect and trouble-free installation. An efficient and attractive outdoor lighting system will enable you to enjoy the garden and patio after dark as well as during the day; for even if it becomes too cold to go outside, the view can be enjoyed from the comfort of your sitting-room or dining-room window. Being able to light the outside can be a useful security advantage, too.

All cables for use outside must be protected by a plastic conduit and buried to a depth of at least 18in (46cm). Where this won't be possible – where a patio has

With their attractive feathery fronds, ferns are a useful foliage plant for shadier areas and a splendid contrast to other fleshier leaf forms. Most prefer shade and a moist soil, being by nature stream-side or woodland. There is a surprising amount of variety within ferns themselves and a group clustered together in a shady area can look very effective. A fern will also do well in a pot providing you do not let the compost dry out. *Dryopteris* are a large group of full to half-hardy ferns including *D. erythrosora* shown here – the Japanese shield fern which grows to around 18in (45cm) and is half-hardy, not dying down until well into winter.

already been installed, for example – cable can be pegged along the top of walls using special fixing clips or slightly recessed into the mortar pointing of a wall. You are advised to enlist the help and advice of a qualified electrician to ensure fitting and fitments are safe. The system should be fitted with an RCB safety circuit breaker which will cut off the power automatically should there be the slightest deviation in the current. Light fittings must be recommended for outdoor use. They vary between 150–300W and there is a limit to how many you can run from a single cable, especially if you are running it some distance from the house which leads to a drop in power levels. A thicker cable or several of them may be the answer if you intend to install a fairly complex system of lights and features. A combination of several different kinds of light is better and creates a more subtle effect than just a few bright, glaring ones. Ideally you should be able to operate some of the lights independently for a choice of effects.

There are various types of garden light producing differing effects. Tungsten has a warm yellow light; discharge lighting is colder with more of a blue-green tinge good for highlighting plants and water features); low-voltage halogen lights produce a very clear white light which shows up flowers and features in their true colours. They all operate through a transformer but one can be used for several lights. Spiked spotlights can be inserted in flower-beds and containers to highlight foliage; clip-on types are useful for fixing to trellis, walls and pergolas as downlighters. As well as highlighting your best plants and features, you need good lighting for sitting, eating and barbecuing in the patio area, taking care to angle the lights correctly so that they do not dazzle. You can buy wall washers which can be used to highlight the best architectural features on your house, and recessed uplighters which are sunk into the ground on a bed of gravel for good drainage and which are protected by toughened safety glass or a special grid, making a very unobtrusive light source.

The best effects rely on the lighting being concealed, but some outdoor lights are more ornamental. Bulkhead lights and lanterns come in a wide range of modern and

Hanging baskets of bright annuals like this *Begonia* are useful for adding colour and interest to house walls, pergolas or indeed anywhere in the garden, using special stands.

traditional styles designed to be fixed to walls or alongside paths and drives. Some are free-standing and you can buy reproductions of the old traditional street lamps. Non-electrical lighting also has its place in the garden. Paraffin lanterns, spiked bamboo flares, candles and nightlights are lovely for romantic meals alfresco or for parties. Some candles will deter insects, too.

Also useful if you have a pool or pond are low-voltage underwater lamps; some fountains are supplied complete with spotlights. If you don't want to have lights under the water, light surrounding features instead and use their reflection to illuminate the pool. Never shine spotlights directly on to the water's surface: it will be too glaring.

Putting on the Style

It may be necessary to reject some features, especially if space is limited, so draw up a shortlist of those you consider essential or are your particular favourites. Your final design decision and one that will affect the

A limited colour scheme is often more effective than a random mix of many colours. It is worth drawing up a planting scheme for a display such as this, shades of purple and mauve highlighted by white and fresh greenery. Remember, foliage is just as good a source of strong colour as blooms.

total look as well as the cost of putting your garden design into practice, is the general style and atmosphere of your new garden. This might take the form of a very definite and disciplined theme such as a blue and white garden in which all the features and flowers are different shades of blue, mauve, white and silver. Alternatively, you may prefer just to capture a certain atmosphere, for example the traditional cottage look with plenty of old favourites among the flowers, such as hollyhocks, lupins, roses and sweet William; plus a wobbly path woven in old brick, or a rustic arch – this would be sufficient to suggest thatch roofs and meadows full of cows even if you lived in the centre of town. Where the garden is a bit of a sun trap why not capture a slice of the Mediterranean with a few terracotta tubs, a collection of aromatic herbs and a bright deckchair?

For those keen on minimalism, an oriental theme might appeal: lots of raked sand, stretches of tranquil water, large and small pebbles all intended to represent larger, natural features such as lakes and mountains. Plants and accessories can be chosen to reinforce your chosen theme: bamboo, grasses, low-growing mosses and sculptured evergreens to create a very formal yet relaxing garden that looks good all year round yet is very simple to maintain. You can buy all manner of oriental-style accessories many of which are based on features traditionally found in the Japanese tea garden, from bamboo deer scarers and fat content Buddhas to little stone lanterns. The secret is not to overdo the effect with too many of these; you should be aiming at a very spare, contemplative atmosphere not a knick-knack grotto.

Drawing up the Plan

To make sure your chosen features look good together and actually fit the site, it is a good idea to draw up a scaled plan. This is quite simply done using squared graph paper and by plotting in the features to a scale of 1:100. On a 1cm grid, each square will equal a metre. This is not only a convenient way of organizing things, but will also make ordering the right amount of materials for paths and paving easier and

Contrary to most design guide-lines, this garden has chosen plants of a similar height and kept strict control over the size and colour of leaves and flowers to create a dense undulating effect as beautiful as a patchwork quilt.

A single accessory or piece of furniture and the right plants can convert the smallest corner into a sweet-scented retreat. Here, pea shingle underfoot and an old table make this small area as practical as it is pretty.

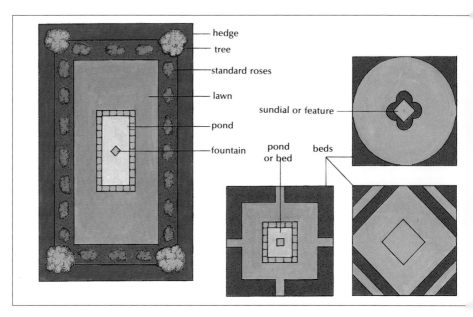

Symmetry is the secret of a formal garden layout and ideally each half of a line drawn latitudinally and longitudinally should be the mirror image of the other. If this is overambitious for your garden, select formal elements and use them as features, maybe screened from the rest of the garden by a fence or screen.

Here is a small informal garden unafraid to exploit every plant's best asset whether that be outsize foliage or the jewel-like fruits of a few apple trees.

more accurate. Under- or over-ordering for these items might be both inconvenient and expensive. You will need to measure the plot accurately by tying a ball of string to a peg and marking it at 3ft (1m) intervals using coloured wool or a marker pen. Start measuring from the house or a boundary wall, working north to south and east to west to measure out the limits of your plot. Draw this up on your graph paper and indicate how the garden is orientated by marking in the north. You can then measure up and plot in accurately the house and any existing immovable features that you will not be changing, such as an existing patio, trees, shrubs and any outbuildings. It is a good idea to photocopy your plan at this stage so that you have several copies to play around with. When you have finished, you can play around with your chosen features

A semi-formal garden plan is far more flexible. It retains a symmetrical layout but some of the elements can be quite informal, producing a much softer look.

until you have a rough idea of how they might work.

Then it is time to move outside again to put stakes in the ground to indicate where your major features will be sited and join them with coloured tape. This will give you some idea of the shape and scale of them *in situ* and help you assess each in relation to surrounding features and the garden as a whole. View them from every angle by walking round the garden and use your imagination to picture these features

completed; check that the sunshine and shade requirements will be correct. If possible, view the whole scheme from one of the upper rooms in the house, too, to give a different, overhead perspective of your plans. Once you are happy with the size and style of each feature it can be plotted in on your master plan.

It is a good idea to mark in a rough idea of the position and spread of major plants as well; you can do this on a separate sheet if it makes things clearer and code them into

This very formal garden divided by concrete paths really comes alive in spring with a canopy of apple blossom and a wallflower carpet. Apple trees are perfect for small gardens, providing both blossom and fruit yet remaining a manageable size.

For a harmonious and successful design you must include house, garden, patio and conservatory if you have one, in your plans. Note how cushion-forming ground-cover plants in pastel shades are the perfect buffer between building and paving, and forge a link with the garden, too.

your main plan. It is possible to buy extra plants and plant them close together, weeding out the extras as they grow for an instantly mature effect but this is a rather expensive way to achieve instant results. Mulching between the plants with chippings or bark chips is a good way to reduce areas of bare earth and help retain moisture until plants have grown.

What you must not do with all the features, though, is to rush out and order the materials straight away; try to live with it for a few days in case you decide to change anything. Only when you are completely happy with your total design should you consider starting constructional work. Here a plan of action is equally valuable; work out the best order for completing features according to what you can afford, the time of year and the most practical sequence in which to do things to minimize work and upheaval. This could save you both money and aggravation.

3 • PATIOS, PATHS AND STEPS

You will surely want to include at least one patio in your plans. A firm, dry level surface is ideal for garden furniture, a barbecue and loungers, a place where you can relax in the sunshine, where the children can play and where you can entertain friends. It is truly an outdoor room and some like to have more than one, each serving a different purpose like rooms in the house. Importantly, the patio should be in the sunniest spot of the garden which is not necessarily by the house, so don't position it there automatically without thinking it through. Although it is convenient being close to the kitchen for serving meals or for opening patio windows or French doors directly on to the garden in warm weather, if the area is permanently chilly or in shade, you are not going to be inclined to use it much and it

would be far better to site the patio in some other part of the garden. In this case, good access from the house via a path or stepping stones is important.

Another consideration is privacy; if the area you have chosen for a patio is overlooked, you should plan for some form of screening, too. Size and shape will be determined by the space available but it is worth making sure that the area you have planned is large enough to take patio furniture and any other features you may have in mind for it.

Bold architectural plants are all very well, but when it comes to finer detail you can't beat the delicate cyclamen, its exquisite butterfly blooms half buried at your feet only managing to catch the eye by means of their jewel-like, glowing colours. Cyclamen need a rich, well-drained soil and will grow in sun or partial shade which makes them good subjects for the outer edges beneath trees. The leaves are often attractive, too, being heart shaped with silver or lighter green patterning. Flowers bloom in spring or autumn and some are sweetly scented. Colours might be white, red, deep pink or purple.

Proving that a patio close by the house need not be a sterile, very formal area, fabulous use of bushy and ground cover plants has created a stunning variety of foliage shapes and colours around and between these old stone slabs.

If you have a balcony, make the most of it with pots and troughs of bright flowers to complement those in the garden below.

Building the Patio

Choice of paving materials is wide and available at varying cost. Perhaps you might like to use a variety of materials to suit different paved areas within your scheme; or combine two or three complementary types as part of a single patio complex. This is a useful device where the paved area is a large one and could benefit from a change

of texture or style to prevent it looking dull or overbearing. Whatever surface you choose, the area must be properly levelled and prepared.

Sometimes it makes sense to terrace the patio, particularly where the ground is uneven and the necessary levelling and backfilling would be a messy and expensive business. A drop of only 6in (15cm) can look effective if the patio is a small one; larger changes in level should incorporate several steps between the two levels. A two-deck patio extends your design possibilities to include a variety of features, for example a waterfall cascading to a pool on the lower level. Whatever final surface you choose, the site must be stripped of topsoil, and levelled. Where the patio adjoins the house, you must take care that the finished level of your patio surface is no less than 6in (15cm) below the damp-proof course. You must also avoid covering up any air vents.

Concrete remains a popular patio surface as it is flexible and relatively easy to lay. Unadorned, it might look a little bleak over large areas but you can colour it with proprietary powders or pattern it to add texture and interest. This might be done by lightly brushing the concrete while still wet to expose the aggregate, applying a special 'stamp' to create standard paving effects, or applying chippings, shingle or coloured stone to the wet surface. Other materials such as cobbles or bricks, mix well with concrete and can be used to create patterns borders and designs.

Paving slabs are by far the favourite form of paving: they come in a wide range of shapes and sizes including squares, rectangles and hexagons, some of which are interlocking to create special patterns and designs. Different colours and textures are available as well as imitations of natural stone and brick, the more expensive versions being quite realistic.

For a country-style patio, natural stone - usually sandstone and limestone - is available as square paving slabs. Sometimes broken pieces are laid down as 'crazy paving'. Although real stone is expensive, second-hand stone and granite setts intended for roadways can sometimes be purchased. They are hard wearing and have an attractive weathered appearance.

For a change of texture in selected areas, gravel and shingle combine well with concrete and paved surfaces. They need to be contained by some kind of edging or they get spread around the rest of the garden. Cobbles are another option that is not really suitable for furniture or comfortable underfoot, but they make an attractive contrast over small areas, particularly around containers. These can be bought in square setts which are as simple to lay as paving slabs. Alternatively, the egg-shaped stones are packed together individually in a bed of mortar or concrete.

Bricks make an attractive patio surface especially if they can be arranged in traditional basketweave and herringbone patterns. Second-hand bricks with their warm, mellow appearance are available from salvage yards and look lovely in a traditional garden or where you wish to create a cottagey feel. New bricks come in a wide range of colours from yellow and buff to reds and blues. Intricate patterns and borders can be used to create sophisticated patio complexes within a more modern garden theme. Bricks are best loosely laid.

Increasingly popular as a garden paving material is timber, which can be laid in the form of decking to create patios, platforms, walkways and bridges. The decking is usually raised at least a few inches from the ground and supported on wooden posts or joists, or fastened to a strong wall with sturdy coach bolts. It is useful for areas that incorporate a change of level as the decking can be raised to any height without the need for expensive levelling and backfilling. Timber's popularity as a construction material in the garden lies in its warm

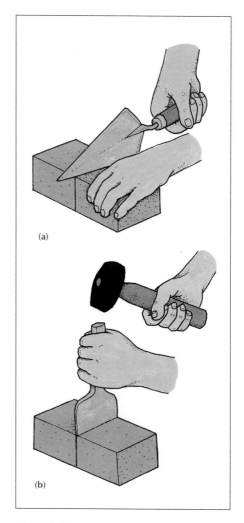

(a)

(b)

Cutting bricks.
(a) Use a broad blade to make a groove along the cutting line.
(b) Place a chisel in the groove and give it a sharp blow with a mallet or bricklayer's hammer.

natural appearance and its flexibility which allows it to follow any shape and design, even to be used to create integral features such as seating, storage and infinite changes of level. Like brick, it can be laid in a variety of geometric patterns; or stained and varnished in shades of russet, blue, grey and green. Decking might be made from Western red cedar or chestnut which are tough and slow to rot; but also from softwoods providing you don't mind treating them annually with a suitable preservative. Both hard and soft timbers must be scrubbed with a rough brush from time to time to remove any slippery fungal growth.

Patio Furniture and Accessories

With patios the design job doesn't finish with laying the paving. It needs furnishing and decorating just like any room in the house, with furniture and accessories in keeping with the style you are aiming to create. Like other garden features, it needs a carefully thought out selection of plants of course, but these will mostly be grown in free-standing containers or built-in beds around the patio. The big difference with patio plants is that they are always in sharp focus and need to look their best all year round. They are often more carefully colour co-ordinated – even when a riot of bright primaries – and keeping some seasonal variety in the display is important, too. If this sounds like a lot of hard work, design a basic plan with a selection of evergreen plants and simply add spring bulbs or summer annuals according to season. Planting up a container liner in advance and dropping it in when it is ready helps keep the display looking at its best at all times.

Your choice of patio furniture will be a great influence on the final look and feel of your patio area. There are also other points to consider before you buy: will it be left

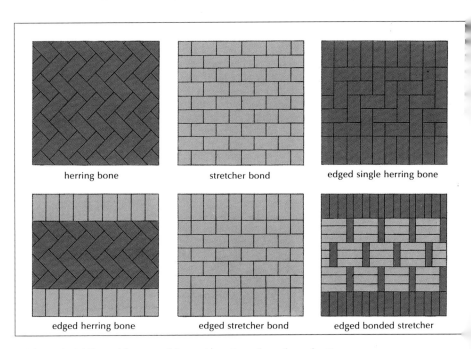

herring bone stretcher bond edged single herring bone

edged herring bone edged stretcher bond edged bonded stretcher

Bricks can be laid in a wide range of decorative patterns for paths and patios.

A superb mosaic design for a very special paved suface.

Choisya ternata, the Mexican orange blossom, is a small garden and patio favourite offering fine evergreen foliage and charming flowers, sometimes blooming in autumn as well as in spring. The shrub makes a good rounded shape about 8ft (2.5m) high and the same across. The leaves are a bright glossy green and are themselves aromatic, studded in spring by clusters of sweet-scented white flowers. It grows best in a sunny position with well-drained soil, and although it is not frost tender it should be given some shelter. You can propagate new plants by taking semi-ripe cuttings in late summer. There is a golden form, *C. ternata* 'Sundance'.

ut all year round or do you prefer the more uxurious but less hardy type of furniture hat must be stored indoors? In this case, ou must make sure you have sufficient torage space in the garage, summerhouse r similar building; or check that the furni-ıre folds away easily.

You will also have to decide how you will be using your patio. Do you want a comfortable place with table and chairs to enjoy a meal and maybe entertain? Or will the patio be a place to relax in so will be furnished with loungers and deckchairs? Families will be looking for inexpensive yet sturdy furniture that can seat plenty of people in the minimum of space, such as the classic solid timber picnic table with integral bench seating. Timber garden furniture can be wonderfully stylish, too: elegant bench seats with decorative backs or designer-made dining furniture that is almost good enough to use indoors. You can still buy antique garden furniture if your patio favours a traditional look; mostly the cast-iron type which is heavily ornate. There are also good cast metal imitations of this style including chairs, tables and love-seats which can be left outside all year round. Some have timber-slatted seats but generally rely on the addition of cushions for comfort. Moulded plastic and aluminium-frame dining furniture is inexpensive and stacks away neatly when not in use.

If comfort is your priority, one of the upholstered ranges will appeal: chairs and

Herbs offer such a lovely collection of foliage shapes and soft colours. They grow as well in containers as they do in the garden; plant them singly or plan a culinary collection in a single, large container.

A collection of sink rock gardens on a pea-shingle patio. Different heights and sizes among the containers make a feature of them as a whole.

loungers usually have moulded plastic frames and sumptuous upholstery in non-fade fabrics, plus foot rests, drinks rests, head rests and all kinds of accessories such as trolleys, tables and mobile bars. This is the kind of furniture that looks most in keeping in a Mediterranean-style setting or on the patio fronting a pool. For an inexpensive yet stylish option for sun worshippers, do not overlook the humble deckchair. It is inexpensive yet smart – re-cover in designer fabric and repaint or re-stain the frame in co-ordinated colours – and it is comfortable, yet folds away easily when not in use.

Non-essential but perfect for giving the patio that individual touch or to reinforce a certain style or atmosphere, are garden ornaments and accessories. Statuary and sculpture are beautiful and may range in size from a small terracotta turtle to a full-scale marble goddess; but a major investment of funds is not necessarily required if you use your imagination. An interesting boulder or piece of driftwood could be used to create an equally fascinating focal point. Small items can be given more prominence by placing them on a low patio wall or positioning them on a plinth or column. If you like symmetrical arrangements, a pair of urns or even stone lions might be just the right thing either side of your patio steps. This is a good way to make an entrance look more imposing. You will find plenty of decorative material at your local garden centre, from sundials and Chinese ginger jars to animal statuettes and ornaments. It is important not to overdo the effect with too many of such items; use them discriminately for maximum impact. Two or three garden ornaments relating to a theme – oriental style for example – can be all that is required to give a patio its theme.

Never underestimate the decorative nature of the plant containers themselves or the patio. These also come in a great many sizes, shapes and materials but, generally speaking, keeping to one kind within a

The dramatic and exotic-looking Yucca likes full sun but it is surprisingly hardy and will grow well as the centre point of your patio scheme, as a contrast to other smaller and rounder-leaved plants in the garden or even in a container providing it receives regular watering. It does not need too heavy a hand with the water as Yuccas prefer a well-drained soil. As well as making a showy clump of tightly packed sword-like leaves up to 6ft (2m) in height, Yucca excels itself when it flowers, too, producing a tall flower stem of white flowers in late summer. The plant can be propagated in spring by division or root cuttings. There are some frost-tender species so do check when you buy.

Matching accessories can be used to bring a scheme together and encourage a relaxed atmosphere. Here white is picked up in decorative urns and statuary to create a very bright, sunny feel among pale stone pavers with white patio furniture, white flowers and variegated foliage.

This old statue has been given a new lease of life for the summer with a cloak of flowering bindweed allowed to grow over her shoulders.

roup looks best. Groups of uneven num-ers, say three or five, seem to make the ost satisfactory composition, maybe in arying heights or sizes. Each container pe has its advantages and own distinctive ook, from ruddy terracotta so redolent of ot Mediterranean courtyards and terraces,

to rustic-style timber barrels, smart timber or wooden and fibreglass Versailles boxes to concrete planters which are available in any size, shape or height. Some containers are designed to serve a particular purpose: hanging baskets to add interest at eye level or above; shallow bowls for low arrangements of seasonal plants; window-boxes to brighten up a dull building; free-standing troughs and sinks for alpine collections.

Paths

The garden path is not simply a means of getting from A to B; it is a most useful design device and one that has to be carefully plotted to obtain maximum impact from its potential. It leads the eye, not just the feet, and by taking a winding route can be used to disguise the shape of the plot or to add an air of mystery by disappearing behind a hedge or screen. From a practical point of view, a path must be level and non-slippery; it links various features around the garden and provides a safe, clean route between them in bad weather. You don't want your path to be too dominant, so try not to position it in full sun – this area is more useful for growing plants in any case.

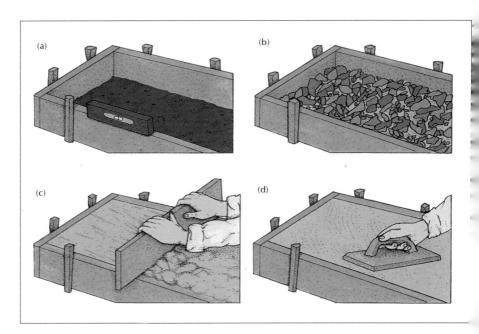

Making a concrete path.
(a)   Excavate the area to a depth of 4–6in (10–15cm) and erect shuttering level with the top of the path. Use a spirit level to ensure it is straight, holding the boards in place with wooden pegs.
(b)   Put in a layer of hardcore up to about 2–3in (5–7.5cm) from the top. Dampen slightly using a watering can.
(c)   Pour on the concrete level with the shuttering and smooth over with a piece of flat-edge timber, pulling it with arms outstretched in a zigzag motion.
(d)   To achieve a fine finish, rub over with a bricklayer's float.

Stepping stones wind their way through a budding jungle of fascinating shapes. With brighter blooms used only as occasional highlights among this clever mass of different shades of green, any sense of a boring, long, narrow garden has been totally obliterated.

Materials used will probably take their lead from other paved features in the garden. If a path still seems too dominant however carefully you design it, consider stepping stones for a more broken, less dominant effect. Slabs, bricks and log slices all make good stepping stone material once bedded into soil or grass. For an informal-style path, do not put cement or sand between bricks or slabs; seeds will wash down between and plants will grow to soften the effect – or you could plant

low-growing plants (for instance, Thyme which doesn't mind being trodden on) of your own choice.

If the garden suddenly encounters a change of level, steps rather than a path or stepping stones will be required. As well as a useful means of getting from one level to another, steps can accentuate the height change and become a feature in their own right. You will find that 4in (10cm) between

A change of level invites a new perspective and the chance to create a separate area within the main garden plan. Here simple steps softened by flowers lead up to a seating area and beyond, to a 'secret' part of the garden partially concealed by shrubs and trees.

each step will be sufficient with the steps themselves around 18in (45cm) deep. This would include a 2in (5cm) overlap. Material used should be the same as that of the retaining walls and other architectural features around the garden. Brick and stone

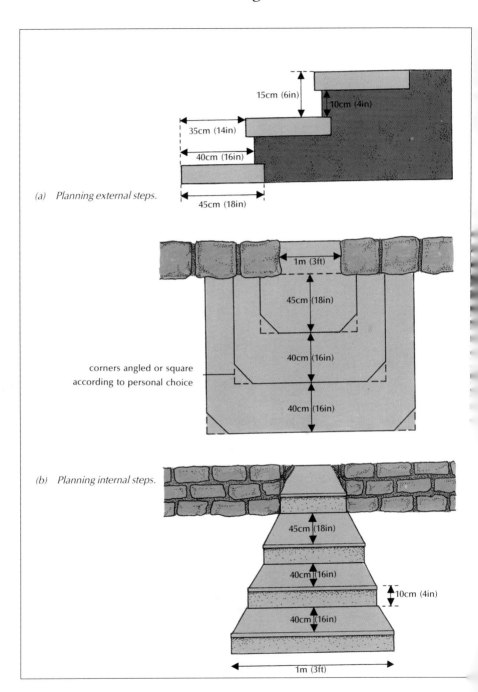

(a) *Planning external steps.*

15cm (6in)

10cm (4in)

35cm (14in)

40cm (16in)

45cm (18in)

1m (3ft)

45cm (18in)

40cm (16in)

corners angled or square
according to personal choice

40cm (16in)

(b) *Planning internal steps.*

45cm (18in)

40cm (16in)

10cm (4in)

40cm (16in)

1m (3ft)

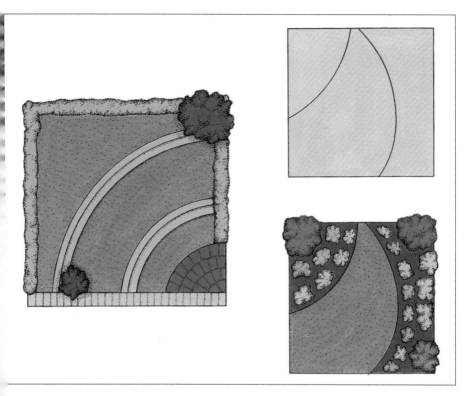

Creating different levels within your scheme adds interest, particularly in a small town garden. It is also a useful device for changing the feel of a square plot especially if you use curved contours and divide the plot diagonally.

are perfect for a very formal look, while timber and rustic poles give a very country feel to the garden. You should begin with the bottom step and work upwards.

Drives

A drive needs to be given more practical thought as it will have to bear a considerable load. Tarmac or concrete are most frequently used, but they are difficult to keep looking good. Cement in particular tends to show every mark and quickly deteriorates rather than maturing to a pleasant mellowness like other garden features. Tough bricks and pavers are more attractive, if expensive, and can be laid in a variety of patterns. A drive can also look more interesting if you brighten it up a little with a few patio features such as tubs of plants or raised beds. If your property is grand enough to have a large or circular drive, a central feature may be natural – a raised bed, pool or statue. Interestingly, any plants you choose to grow in a border alongside a driveway will grow better than if grown beside a lawn, the reason being that extra water runs off the surface of the drive and collects on the underside of the stone.

4 • PLANTING BEDS AND LAWNS

All too often, planting beds are not properly planned or drawn up. They start off as a good idea with a little bit carved off here, a modification to the shape there, resulting in a vague kind of curve that bears no real relation to the form and design of the rest of the garden. For that professional landscaped look every element must be an integral part of the whole. Think seriously when drawing your scale plan as to how plants are going to fit into the scheme of things, what kind of plants they will be (see Chapter 6) and how they could be best displayed. Containers, as discussed in the previous chapter, have the big advantage of being flexible: you can move them around and change the display quite easily, even replant or replace the soil if needs be. Permanent beds are a completely different matter. Their size and shape must relate directly to other shapes and features in the garden; often you will be aiming for a collection of plants that will mature over the years, not simply be in for a season.

The bed shapes must be boldly sketched, with no fiddly corners, they should be accessible and, above all, easy to maintain. Borders are no longer regimented bands that run the length of the garden, packed with herbaceous material that needs staking, trimming and rejuvenating. They snake sinuously into the distance, confusing the eye as to exactly how long or wide the garden really is. Very little bare soil is to be seen thanks to clever choice of plants, plenty of ground-covering varieties and easy-care mulching techniques.

There is a greater variety of beds, too: not just describing informal shapes even within a formal plan or structure, but dramatic island beds that act as a diversion or as a screen enhancing the remainder of the garden as an unseen mystery (even if it is only the potting shed or the dustbins).

Raised beds on the patio as a fully integrated part of the patio design, offer the chance to enjoy plants at waist level – ideal

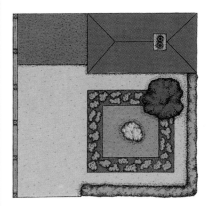

(a)

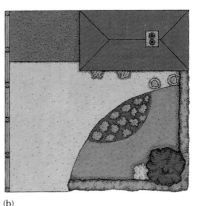

(b)

(a) A boring and predictable way to treat a small rectangular front garden. The formal design of the planting beds is too square and difficult to maintain with a central Camellia making it look fussy and crowded. The tree is planted too near the house and is likely to create problems with shade and invasive roots.
(b) A far more attractive design for the same plot. The tree and shade-tolerant Camellia are grouped together in the far corner to provide a sensible backdrop for a curved area of lawn and an easy-care heather garden. This way you seem to get more of everything because the drive is enlarged, too.

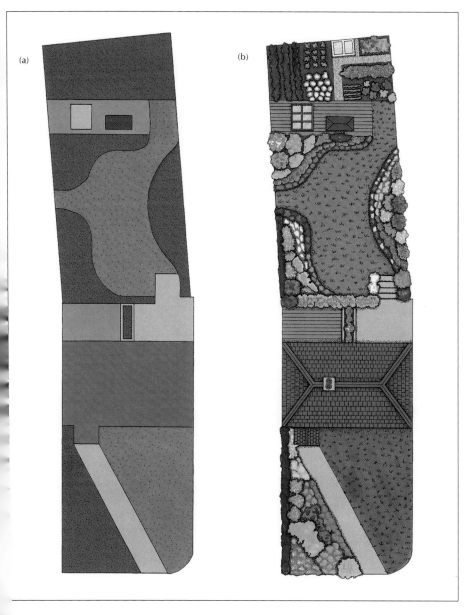

(a)   Your initial plan drawing will show the shape and size of your garden site with all the existing features you intend to keep and around which you can plot in the basic framework.
(b)   The finished plan shows how informal planting beds disguise the rectangular shape of the plot and hide the vegetable area.

for small-leaved or scented species or for disabled gardeners. Such beds can be made to any shape depending on the type of material you intend to face them with: trying to surround an irregular shape with bulky railway sleepers (railroad ties) for example, is just a way to make life difficult for yourself. The beds are generally 18–24in (45.5–60cm) deep with drainage holes left in the sides at ground level. If this is likely to cause a problem with water staining the patio surface, a gulley will have to be constructed to carry the water away at patio construction stage. The beds can be made from bricks, timber, stone or ornamental walling blocks depending on the style of the rest of the patio. They should incorporate a layer of rubble or shingle in the bottom for drainage, topped by a good light to medium topsoil or potting compost. In raised beds you can adjust the soil to suit your plants: plenty of acidic compost if the bed is for growing lime-hating plants; a free-draining soil for alpines or bulbs. If you like the idea of raised beds or find them a particularly practical option, feel free to incorporate them in your plans for the rest of the garden. They are perfect for containing herbs or vegetables where space is limited or the general theme formal.

Summer-flowering bulbs are the garden's bonus – once planted they need very little attention yet they reward the gardener with a wonderful display of lush blooms, many of which are suitable for enhancing the home as well as the flower border. Lilies are especially lovely and there are many different varieties to choose from offering the most glorious forms and colours, many delightfully scented too (although attractive red *L. amabile* smells dreadful). As well as the classic lily white, the waxy blooms may be red, yellow, purple, brown, orange, pink, blue, cream or yellow with all manner of stripes, spots and blotches. Few plants can offer such rewards for little more than plenty of sunshine and a well-drained soil.

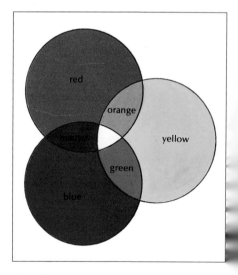

The colour spectrum. You can see how colour harmonies work by observing where the primary shades overlap. Thus you can be confident blending blues and greens, yellow and orange, yellow and green and so on.

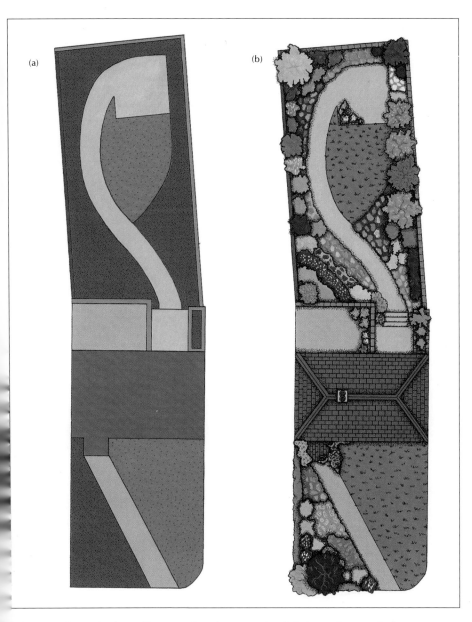

(a)

(b)

A long thin plot needs plenty of interest at the sides using a detailed planting framework of trees, shrubs and smaller plants to give the impression of depth. A curving path arranged across the diagonal makes an attractive focal point and also serves to make the garden look wider than it really is.

Beautiful Lawns

As with your planting beds, it is important that your lawn, should you be having one, is not just a square or rectangle stuck in the middle of the plot, but a properly planned feature, shaped to complement the general garden design. Experiment with shapes on your scaled plan, remembering that the area must be easy to mow and that you need access for the mower. Of course, an area of neatly trimmed grass is not obligatory although it has been a feature of most gardens since their earliest history. You might plan for areas of gravel to create a change of colour and texture; or grow an old fashioned herb lawn such as thyme or chamomile. It might not be as neat as a piece of velvet, but it will smell wonderful

underfoot and, once established, is less of a chore to maintain.

Often the garden has an existing lawn and even if this is in a state of some neglect, it is usually worth restoring if it suits your plans rather than digging it over and starting again. A mature lawn takes some time to

Lungwort (*Pulmonaria*) is a wonderfully useful foliage plant with the bonus of pretty blue flowers in spring. While the tubular flowers are small and delicate, almost like those of a wild plant, the leaves are quite dramatic: very green and lance shaped with distinctive spotted white markings. This perennial plant's big advantage is that it prefers shady positions and is not fussy about its soil, as long as it is moist. It will thrive where very little else will grow easily. Some are semi-evergreen reducing to a small rosette of leaves over winter; it is certainly one of the earliest plants to start making a display in the garden, long before the frosts are finished.

Hardy houseleeks (*Sempervivum*) make a dense mat of curious fleshy rosettes in shades of yellow, green, dark red and purple. Because they prefer a free-draining, stony soil and plenty of sun, they thrive in alpine banks, on walls, scree gardens and even on the low-tiled roof of a shed or outhouse. The plants are evergreen and take several years to reach flowering size; the flowers themselves are star shaped. The rosettes die back after the plant has flowered but it regenerates itself through the many offsets it produces. New plants can be propagated in the same way. Houseleeks make a useful contrast to other, more delicate alpine plants.

Beautiful beds and borders rely on a good variety of foliage shapes and bushy, healthy plants. Estimating the approximate spread and height of each plant in your planting plan and positioning them accordingly are also guaranteed to get good results.

establish. You will find that, after a while, regular mowing of a lawn that has started to look a bit shaggy will reduce the coarser grasses and restore it to a finer finish. Worn areas will have to be patched by forking over the damaged area during the growing season, sieving the soil to remove any stones or perennial weeds (topping up with quality loam if necessary), then firming down and planting with lawn seed at the rate of 20oz/sq yd (50g/sq m). Cotton thread

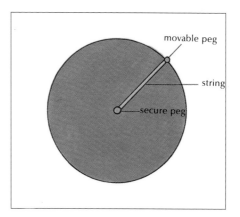

To mark out a circular feature, you must drive a strong metal or wooden peg attached to a piece of string into the ground where you want the centre of your circle to be. Cut the string to the diameter of your proposed circle and attach another peg to this end. With the string taut, you can mark out your circle. Semi-circles can be used to draw scalloped effects.

A small but well-planned plot with attention focused around a grass area. A mixture of curved and angular features is well blended. The specimen tree is birch (Betula).

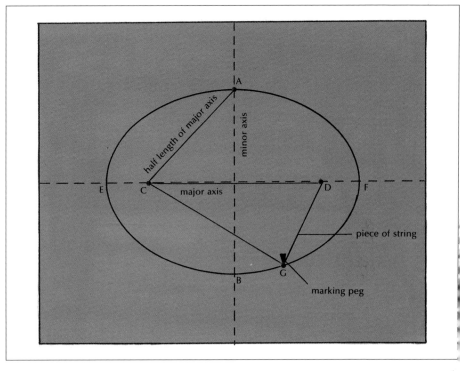

The method for marking out an oval can be adapted to all curved edges. You must mark a cross with the lines at right angles to each other at the centre point. The cross will have two identical short sides being the width of your shape, and two longer ones to make up the length. This will give you a major and a minor axis. To mark out the oval you need two centres of curvature. To find these, place a peg at point A and, with a piece of string half the length of the major axis, mark an arc to cut the major axis at two points: C and D. Fix two pegs at C and D as anchor points. With another piece of string measuring twice the length of the distance from D to E (the farthest point of your proposed oval), make a loop making sure you don't use up any of your measured length to make the knot. The loop is hooked over pegs D and C and a sharp pointed peg inside the loop at G used to mark out the shape from G to B and then E. This procedure is repeated on the other side to mark A to F to G.

stretched across the area will discourage birds from eating the seed. Edges are usually patched by cutting turves as necessary and turning them round so that the freshly cut edge is to the outside. The bald area on the inside can then be treated as just described.

A few weeds in the lawn won't really matter unless you are a perfectionist as long as they stay green; but you may have so many that they will have to be treated. Perennial weeds with a crown, such as dandelions and some plantain, can be sprinkled with sulphate of ammonia or a little table salt to kill them. Take care not to spill too much on the surrounding grass and do not use in any large quantities.

Most lawns tend to become compacted

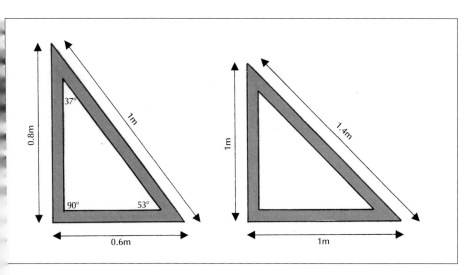

A set square is useful for getting the angles right for geometric shapes within your plan.

and it is worth aerating the soil to encourage the finer grass cultivars to flourish. The surface should be scarified with a long-toothed lawn rake in the autumn to remove thatching and a fork inserted into the soil to about 2–3in (5–8cm) depth every 12in (30cm) to aerate the roots. To boost growth, feed the lawn with a proprietary fertilizer in spring. Watering is recommended during dry spells to keep the grass green but don't worry too much if there are water restrictions in your area: the grass recovers surprisingly well even after turning brown.

Should it be necessary to create a new lawn from scratch, you will have to wait until spring or autumn before new grass can be planted. Turfing the new lawn produces instant effects but is more expensive and not always totally successful. The ground should be levelled and any traces of rubble removed before covering with new topsoil. The area should be well drained, laying drainage pipes if necessary. The topsoil is then raked completely level, checking with plank and spirit level, and the area seeded with the lawn mixture of your choice: some mixtures are tougher than others for harder use, such as a family lawn, and will contain ryegrass. The best way to ensure even distribution of seed is to divide the area into 1yd/1m squares, sowing 20oz/sq yd (50g/sq m) into each square. A plank beside the square is useful to stand on and prevents compacting the soil. Weigh out your first 20oz (50g) and mark the level on a can or pot. The seeded area will have to be protected from birds with a network of cotton fixed to pegs. The grass receives its first cut when it is around 2.5in (6cm) tall. It is important not to wear heavy boots and to have the mower at its highest setting.

To turf a lawn, you must start at some accurate point of reference such as the house wall and put in a base line. The first row of turves will be laid to form a straight edge against your base string. To start the second row, you cut a turf in two and start with a half to stagger the turves and give them strength. A plank is essential to avoid compression of the soil. Turves must be watered religiously until they have established a proper root system.

5 • WATER FEATURES

However simple, whatever its size, a water feature adds a touch of magic to any garden or patio design. The smallest pond acts like a mirror reflecting the movement of sky and surrounding trees and plants; a moving water feature such as a fountain or wall-mounted water spout produces delightful sounds as well as sparkle and splash. Although they may take a little time and trouble to install, water features make a superb focal point, look good for most of the year and need very little maintenance. You should try to fit one into your plan somewhere, if not as a major feature, perhaps to liven up an otherwise uninteresting corner. To look in keeping, plan it not in isolation but in conjunction with some other feature such as a patio complex or a rockery.

Ponds

A pond or pool can be informal: a rough kidney shape with an interesting variety of plants where wildlife will quickly collect; or a raised formal type might be more suitable: a smart square, rectangle or circle bordered by stone, brick or slabs to match your paving surface. It could be any size, from no more than a bowl to a complete pool complex covering a large part of your plot area, crossed by timber walkways and incorporating raised patios and built-in planting beds. Always make it as big as you can afford, in terms of space and cost, as you will soon become seduced by the prospect of wonderfully dramatic water plants, fish and other watery accessories and wish you had more scope. The right position is more important; it must be reasonably sunny for water plants to flourish and away from any trees or plants likely to be a nuisance with dropping leaves at the end of summer.

To make a sunken pool, first mark out the shape using pegs and string or a length of

Even the smallest garden can enjoy a garden pond. Here, hidden away among a beautifully blended collection of plants and subtly coloured flowers, only a gleam and the flicker of brightly coloured fish reveal a tiny stone-surrounded pool.

hosepipe. When you are happy it is right, the hole can be excavated, with a spade if it is really small; but anything larger requires a mechanical digger which you can hire by the day or the weekend. It is important to make sure you have suitable access for such a machine. The hole should be dug and levelled, including a ledge about 6in (15cm) below the proposed surface to stand marginal plants on. Any stones or sharp objects must be removed and the inside covered in a layer of sand, then sacking, old carpet or a proprietary pond under-lining material.

There are various ways to line a pool. You can buy ready-shaped fibreglass moulds in a wide variety of sizes and shapes and if you do find one that fits the kind of look you are trying to create, it is a very quick and convenient way of creating a water feature. In this instance, you dig a hole to fit the shape of the mould, only slightly larger, prepare as described, then lower it gently into the hole. It is essential to check that the pool is level and this can be done by placing a plank across the top and using a spirit level. Packing damp sand between the mould and your excavations will ensure a snug fit; this is important, or the weight of water might cause the mould to distort and break.

For a more individual shape and size, rubber or plastic pool-lining material is the most popular. You buy this off the roll or in packs to fit and the pressure of water stretches it to fit the hole. Butyl rubber is the most expensive of these materials but it is stronger and has a longer life. You can repair it, too.

To calculate the size of liner you will need, measure twice the depth plus the length of your excavated pool and add 2ft (60cm). The width will be twice the depth plus the width and 2ft (60cm). The liner is placed over the pool and weighted along the banks with bricks or smooth boulders, then water is allowed to fill the pool slowly through a hosepipe. You adjust the lining as it fills, smoothing out any creases and making tucks as required.

The traditional way to line a pool is to concrete it, and this is certainly long lasting and strong. However, you do need to have some previous experience of using concrete to get it right and the lining is prone to cracking in winter, even with frost-proof additives. Measurements must be accurate: the base and sides ought to be at least 6in (15cm) thick, so allow for this when you dig out the hole. To work out how much concrete will be required, you will have to add up the total area of the base and sides and multiply by the thickness of the concrete. Remember to subtract the thickness of the base from the height of the sides and the thickness of the walls from the length of the two sides opposite. The concrete mix must be one part cement to two parts sand and three parts coarse aggregate (gravel or crushed stone). You can measure the parts accurately in a bucket or wheelbarrow.

Lay your concrete when there is no risk of frost or hot weather which will dry it out too quickly. The sides of the pool will have to be reinforced with crumpled chicken wire,

With their distinctive pleated foliage and range of interesting colours and patterns, Hostas – sometimes called Plantain Lilies – are a splendid designer's foliage plant. They thrive in rich, moist soil so are often seen close to ponds and other water features but also do equally well in pots and tubs providing the compost is kept well watered. Hostas are hardy and grow in shade, making them a very useful ground-covering plant; they produce a large, dense clump anything from 5in (12cm) to 3ft (1m) high, depending on type. The flowers, which are considered secondary, are actually quite attractive, the pale mauve or blue trumpets carried on long stems. The leaves are definitely dominant: thick and flashy with their deep indented markings and a range of colours from blue and grey to dark green and gold. Some have contrasting edges or a different colour on the underneath of the leaves. Hostas are prone to slug and snail damage so take preventative action.

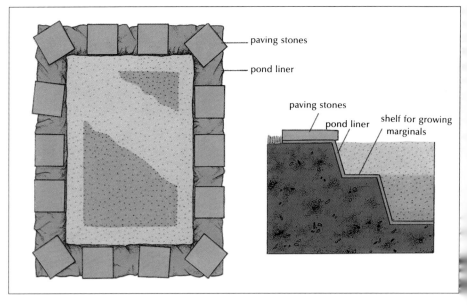

paving stones

pond liner

paving stones

pond liner

shelf for growing marginals

Constructing a sunken pond with a flexible liner. The liner is held in position with slabs or stones and the weight of the water pulls it into place. The lining material should be folded and adjusted as the pond fills.

making sure there are no air pockets in or around it. If you are building a formal pool, you will need timber shuttering around the sides, too. Rub these with a soapy cloth so that they can be removed after the concrete has set. Pouring the concrete between the shuttering and the sides of the pool takes skill; the mix must be stiff enough not to slump to the bottom. It will take weeks to harden, but the pool can be filled with water after around 24 hours providing you do not stand in it or disturb it in any way for three or four days.

You will not be able to stock the pool with plants or fish until the lime content of the concrete has been flushed away. This is done by emptying and refilling the pool four to six times over a period of several weeks. If you are impatient to use the pool straight away, there is a sealant you can paint on to it; this does wear away eventually but by

this time the risk is sufficiently diminished not to be a problem.

A raised pool is the perfect addition to a patio; it creates a change of level and can be extended to include seating, raised planting beds and other features. Because of the pressure of water, a double liner is needed: with butyl rubber or PVC by preference as the exposed conditions make concrete too prone to frost damage. A regular geometric shape such as a square, circle or rectangle is easier to construct, especially if you make sure the design can be constructed from a complete number of bricks or blocks to save cutting.

Approximate the size of the finished pool and divide the length and width of the structure by the length of one of the brick or blocks. A few extra should be allowed for breakages. Double the length and width gives you the number of bricks necessary for a single course and you can estimate the total number of courses by dividing the height of the pond by the height of your brick or block. The liner is tucked into the top course making this the final level of the water. The inner wall could be built from plain concrete blocks as it won't be seen; these will be calculated in the same way. You mark out the pool as for a sunken type with pegs and string, making sure any corners are correct by measuring the diagonals, which should be of equal length. The foundations will be dug to below the level of the topsoil so that the concrete base lies below ground level and can be extended beyond the line of the walls for stability. Once the foundations have been compacted and levelled, pegs can be installed removing them before the concrete sets), checking for accuracy with a spirit level.

Although it makes sense to build the inner wall first, it is a good idea to lay at least one course of the outer wall to indicate the size and position of the finished pool. A circular raised pool is possible but it requires a little more skill and cannot be double skinned as the bricks do not align properly. If you are only looking for a small feature, perhaps you could consider creating a small raised pond from a waterproofed barrel or circular planter.

Bog Gardens

A bog garden is far more exciting than it sounds; in the kind of waterlogged, rich soil usually found around the perimeters of ponds and alongside streams, a fabulous variety of plants flourish, from feathery astilbes and the beautiful Globe Flower (*Trollius*), to giants such as the huge *Gunnera manicata* with its leaves like umbrellas. You can create a small free-standing bog garden in an old tub or container with suitable holes for drainage. It could be sunk into the ground or remain on a patio or

The giant *Gunnera manicata* is mostly seen growing close by a pond or pool or in a bog garden, as it prefers a rich, damp soil. With mature plants making a massive clump 6ft (2m) tall by 7ft (2.2m) wide of huge prickly edged leaves, it is a landscape architect's favourite. Each leaf might be as big as 5ft (1.5m) across and a deep green colour. In a sunny position, the plant produces pale green flower spikes in spring which develop into orange-brown seed pods by late summer. Where there is a chance of hard frosts in winter, the plant needs some kind of protection in the form of a mulch; usually some of the giant leaves are folded down over the crown as it dies back.

paved surface. A more natural effect can be created by extending one side of an informal pond into a boggy area. This also serves a useful purpose as an overflow facility for the pond. You might even prefer to have a bog garden rather than a pond since you get all the fun of the plants without the cost and upheaval of any excavations. It is safer for children, too.

A shallowly dug area – or a natural damp depression – is lined with punctured PVC or butyl liner to maintain a level of around 3in (7.5cm) of water on top of the soil. To keep the soil this waterlogged, you will probably have to keep it topped up with a hose; a useful tip is to insert a length of plastic pipe with holes punched in it into the bottom before the bog garden is planted up. The other end should be easy to hide behind nearby foliage.

Moving Water Features

A fountain, cascade or waterfall can be used to enhance a pool and make it into a much more complex, interesting feature. But they can also be employed as features in their own right. This can be a particularly useful device where the garden is used by young children since the reservoir of water can be hidden underground so there is no risk of drowning. You will need a pump; these have varying capacities so it is important to buy one big enough to do the job, especially if you are expecting it to run several features such as a fountain and watercourse. Pumps may be above ground in which case they need some kind of waterproof housing sited unobtrusively, close to the water; or they may be submersible which means they can operate under the water. The submersible type is more expensive but is easier to maintain and you can keep it running in winter to keep the water free from ice.

Sometimes a feature suggests itself; a waterfall in conjunction with a rockery, for example. It can take some time to get the

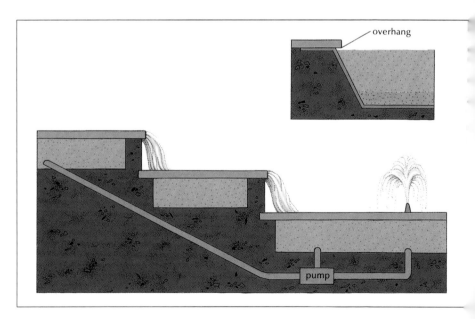

A pump offers the opportunity to create all kinds of exciting moving water features. This formal three-deck cascade makes the most of a slight slope and includes a small fountain in the bottom pool.

water running over the boulders in a realistic matter; lining behind the rocks with pool-lining material prevents the water from disappearing down the back. Sometimes a perspex lip at the head of the falls produces a better effect as it prevents back trickling. Contemporary versions of the waterfall are available if yours is a more modern garden scheme. The water might cascade down an ornamental (waterproofed) wall, or over sheer perspex. The number of creative ideas are limitless, from a sophisticated arrangement where a cascade joins two pools on different levels, to simple waterspouts where the water trickles from a wall-mounted head or similar device into a small bowl.

Fountains come in all shapes and sizes, from basic plumes to cascading bell shapes and sprays. There are all kinds of ornamental statuary, too, designed to be used in conjunction with a fountain device. The important thing to consider (besides good taste!) is whether the fountain will splash or overspill its pool or container; you don't want to be constantly topping up the water levels. One of the prettiest ideas for the patio or a corner of the garden is a bubble fountain. Here the water plays over a series of cobblestones or a large brass ball, sometimes an old stone millwheel before filtering into an underground reservoir to be recycled to the top of the feature again.

Plants for Water Gardens

Everyone who has a pond wants at least one water-lily; they do spread quickly to cover the water's surface so unless yours is a large pool, you will be restricted to one or two. There are a great many varieties to choose from including many colours and forms, so take your time deciding which you like best. Water-lilies require a rich compost and an open mesh container which is positioned at the bottom of the pond so that the leaves float naturally on the surface of the water. When they start to smother the surface of the pond, they must be thinned out, preferably in May before growth really gets going. Other, less exotic-looking plants which float on the water's surface include the beautiful water hyacinth, *Eichhornia crassipes*, which produces superb spikes of scented blue flowers, the tiny-leaved Frogbit, *Hydrocharis morsus-ranae* which spreads quickly and produces tiny white flowers, and the floating heart (*Nymphoides*). These are plants which need no anchorage but whose roots float freely in the water.

For your marginal shelf choose from a wide range of dramatic plants that will efficiently disguise the edge of the pond and blend its outline into other garden features, as well as put on a good display of foliage and flowers. These can be placed in special underwater planting baskets to be balanced on the marginal shelf or positioned where the roots will be around 2–6in (5–15cm) below water. Baskets help inhibit rampant growth; cover the top of the soil with a layer of pea shingle to prevent fish disturbing the soil and polluting the water. The plants can simply be planted directly on the shelf with a few stones to keep them slipping off if you prefer.

Aim for a good variety of foliage shape, size and colour as well as flowers. Iris are stately and elegant, water forget-me-nots (*Myosotis palustris*) make a cushion of tiny blue flowers. *Typha* (reedmace) is the one that looks like a bullrush, ideal for the rear of arrangements while *Sagittaria sagittifolia* has glossy green leaves shaped like an arrowhead. Bog plants can be equally exciting, from the outsized *Gunnera manicata* and Rheum to the textured plants and bright stripes of the Hostas and the stunning arum-like Lisichiton. In these lush, rich conditions, all of these will grow out of hand if not reduced in size before clumps get too large.

6 • DESIGNING WITH PLANTS

A well-designed framework and attractively constructed features may be the key to a successful garden design, but it is the soft landscaping – the plants – that bring it to life and offer most fun in choosing an exciting balanced display. The beauty of this kind of 'exterior decorating' is that it changes and develops all the time with the seasons and it is so easy to create a totally different look simply by substituting a different species or new range of varieties. There is such a wealth of shapes, sizes and colours that almost anything is possible, providing you always pay attention to each plant's particular needs and give it the soil/climate conditions it needs to thrive. Whether you like single colour themes or a riotous blaze, it is close attention to contrasting shapes and heights that gives a planting scheme depth and interest. Trees, shrubs and evergreens can be used to create a basic, easily maintained framework with additional plants filling in the gaps to provide seasonal interest. It is possible to have something going on all year round if you just plan it carefully.

It is a good idea to put your planting plan down on paper so that you can see how well the plants go together and you will also find this a very handy buying guide, especially if you won't be buying all the plants at the same time. You don't have to be artistic with your plan – just a circle or irregular shape showing the average spread of the plant with its name scribbled inside is fine. You could colour the patches with pens or pencils if you want to experiment with a sophisticated colour scheme. Single colour schemes have become popular: all white flowers balanced by green and silver foliage; or yellow blooms co-ordinated with gold and green leaves. Adding more variety, you will find certain colour combinations work better than others: blues, mauves and pinks, for example; yellows creams and oranges. Reds are so vivid and eye-catching, they are best kept for

No garden is complete without at least one rose and there's a type to meet almost any design requirement: ground cover, climbers, tree, bush, even miniature varieties. Roses are generally grown for their superb blooms and a good display can be encouraged by feeding the plant every three weeks through spring and summer. The glossy, distinctly shaped foliage is a perfect foil for the flowers and, from the many hundreds of hybrids available, almost any colour is possible as well as single, semi-double, double and fully double forms. Shown here is *R.* 'Silver Jubilee' which is one of the more modern varieties, a dense bush type producing a mass of large salmon-pink blooms as big as 5in (12cm) across with over 30 petals on each flower. Flowering freely right through the summer, this slightly scented rose makes an upright bush about 3½ft (1.1m) tall with a 2½ft (75cm) spread of glossy leaves.

occasional splashes of bright colour to create a seasonal focal point.

Your scheme will need height and that can be provided not just by trees, but also by climbing plants which can be trained over fence, trellis, pergola and other free standing supports. Climbers make excellent screening material, too, and you can control the effect by choosing evergreen or deciduous types depending on whether you need the cover all year round. Ivies are one of the most versatile evergreen climbers and the *Hedera helix* hybrids include a wonderful variety of shapes and colours, from tiny arrowheads and heart shapes to bright golds, creams and greens. Many climbing plants produce beautiful scented flowers, not just in summer but in winter as well. The delicate Winter Jasmine is every bit as lovely as summer's Honeysuckle or Clematis, and is perhaps valued all the more for being so lovely when little else is stirring. For a cottage-style garden, a selection of scented climbers is obligatory: the rambling rose smothering a rustic trellis with blooms in mid-summer is surely quintessential. In

A skilful blend of deep greens, pinks and purples has created a very enjoyable harmony of plant shapes and sizes.

An outstanding seasonal plant can be used as a focal point and feature in its own right. Ivy-leaved pelargoniums have a trailing habit which makes them perfect for growing in containers. As well as the attractive foliage, they are free flowering to create a splendid display.

the small garden, trees are more likely to be used as a special feature or focal point and there are quite a few decorous types that make an excellent display and won't overshadow the rest of the garden. Japanese maples, the *Acer palmatum*, offer delightfully shaped foliage and gorgeous autumn colour; the crabapple, Malus, is another good-value small tree with attractive foliage, beautiful blossom and colourful fruits, too. Other trees you might choose for smaller gardens include ornamental cherries (Prunus), Laburnam, elegant Birch and glossy Holly.

Shrubs add depth to your scheme, offer an excellent variety of interesting evergreen and deciduous foliage, and provide special seasonal highlights with their wonderful variety of blooms. Many of their flowers are so striking that you have to be careful not to create too many jarring contrasts: some of the Azaleas, for example, can be almost fluorescent. Shrubs can be used for background planting, as a screen or even as a focal point. Some will even tolerate shade which makes them useful for filling those awkward corners that don't receive much sunshine: pretty Cotoneaster, reliable

The lovely Passion Flower (*Passiflora*) looks so unusual and exotic, it is difficult to believe it can be grown outdoors in temperate climates. Some varieties are frost tender and will do better in a conservatory, but half-hardy types will flourish in any fertile, well-drained soil in full sun or partial shade. The Passion Flower is a tendril climber and most types are vigorous growers requiring plenty of water during the growing season. Stems will need supporting and thinning out after the spurt of growth in spring. Every part of the plant is attractive from the evergreen/semi-evergreen leaves to the incredible flowers with their strange central filaments and, often, orange-yellow round or oval fruits in autumn which are edible. Passion Flower can be propagated by seed or from semi-ripe cuttings in summer.

Putting on the Style

Sometimes an attractive and well-planned scheme isn't enough. You may also be aiming to create a most definite feel or atmosphere in your garden or modest back-yard: a kind of fantasy or restful retreat from the hurly burly of the real world outside. Many town dwellers long for a real old-fashioned country garden and this is easily achieved if you choose plants and features carefully. Keep the hard landscaping infor-mal and natural – avoid any hard lines or angles and go for second-hand timber or stripped rustic poles for any constructional features. A rambling rose or two, holly-hocks, pansies, stocks, with a few herbs and vegetables mixed in . . . add a sensible garden bench to sit and enjoy it all and that should easily conjure up the right feel.

Never underestimate the importance of underplanting – a carpet of tiny flowers or foliage is always more attractive than bare earth and helps preserve moisture, too. Underplanting is particularly important beneath spring bulbs and leggy rose bushes.

Viburnum and the stunning Camellia for instance. Against this strong and reliable background will be your seasonal plants to provide an ever-changing display of interest from the very first spring bulbs – plant them in swathes or clumps of a single kind for the most stunning effect – to summer's profu-sion of bright bedding plants and stately perennials. You will know your own favourites: check the latest seed catalogues for new introductions and new colours.

If the garden or patio is a bit of a suntrap you may prefer to bring back memories of happy holidays with a Mediterranean theme. Grey and silver foliaged plants and plenty of bright-coloured blooms such a

You can buy decorative patio blocks for building ornamental walls, seating and other built-in patio features.

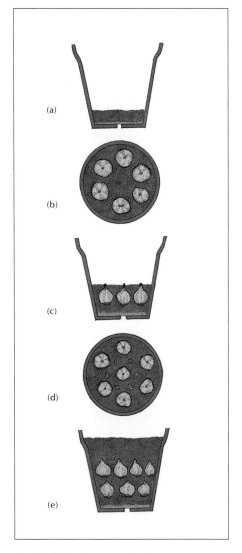

begonias, busy lizzies and geraniums in pots, tubs and hanging baskets should generate a hot, happy atmosphere even when the sun is not shining. Choose terracotta for pots and accessories, ceramic tiles or mosaic to pave the patio if you can guarantee it will be frost free, a large umbrella and some elegant patio furniture and you will need nothing more than a bottle of wine and a bowl of olives to be immediately transported to the Continent.

By contrast, the oriental style of gardening is almost austere but extremely restful. It looks particularly good where the home interior has a similar theme and the interior can merge effortlessly with the exterior. Planned mainly around a strong framework

Planting bulbs for a patio display.
(a) About 2in (5cm) of bulb fibre is placed in the bottom of the container.
(b) Arrange a layer of bulbs on top.
(c) Cover the bulbs with fibre so that the tips protrude.
(d) Plant a second layer of bulbs between the heads of the first.
(e) Top up with bulb fibre for a massed display.

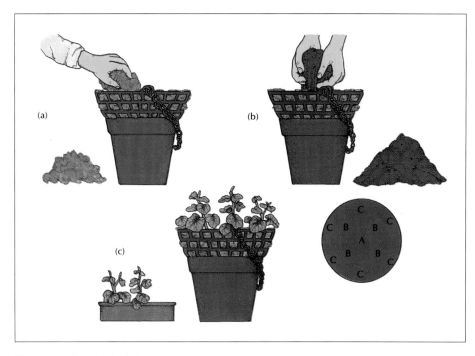

Planting up a hanging basket.
(a) Place basket over a pot for ease of filling and line it with moss or a preformed liner.
(b) Fill with potting compost and water carefully to wet the mixture thoroughly.
(c) Plant up with suitable plants, firming them into the compost. A will be your tallest specimen, B something short and bushy, C a trailing plant.

of simple stone and timber features with closely cropped evergreens and tranquil pools or delicate water features, the Japanese garden has the advantage of looking good in winter as well as the rest of the year. Among the muted greens, greys and browns, strong colour is reserved for occasional seasonal highlights such as the blaze of a cherry or Azalea in spring and summer or the glow of dwarf maple leaves in autumn. Designed to imitate the natural landscape in miniature, rocks, pebbles, water, sand and moss can be used to create some very beautiful effects. Once it has been constructed, this style of garden is much easier to handle than the traditional formal garden which relies on almost constant care and attention to keep it in prime condition. Some of the burden of maintenance can be reduced by use of clipped evergreens, ground-cover plants and hard landscaping rather than areas of lawn.

Success with a formal garden relies on a strong basic plan, probably involving symmetrical features and lots of geometric patterns. Planting beds will be sharply defined and weed free, the plants themselves of uniform shape and size, being changed four times a year to maintain peak condition and interest. Topiary subjects are perfect for this style of garden, box or yew being clipped into formal shapes and designs. You can

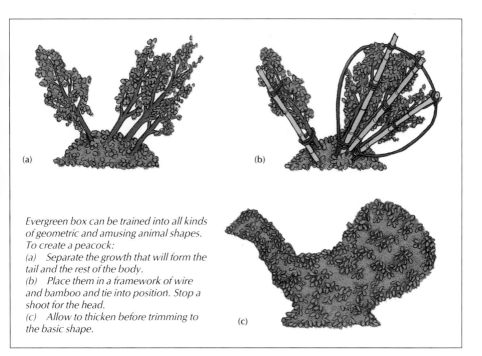

(a)

(b)

Evergreen box can be trained into all kinds of geometric and amusing animal shapes. To create a peacock:
(a) Separate the growth that will form the tail and the rest of the body.
(b) Place them in a framework of wire and bamboo and tie into position. Stop a shoot for the head.
(c) Allow to thicken before trimming to the basic shape.

(c)

buy these ready shaped or, if you have the time and patience, create your own. Another way to create large decorative features is to grow trees as standards: a long single stem topped by a ball of foliage plus flowers, fruit, berries as appropriate. This treatment particularly suits citrus trees (which will need warmth and shelter during the colder months) but can also be successful with holly, marguerites and fuchsia.

Rock Gardens

Creating a rock garden is a wonderful opportunity to grow and observe the delightful variety and form of alpine plants. The area need not be large – a stone sink on the patio makes a lovely feature – but if you do have a natural slope or rocky outcrop this is a wonderful way to use it. Alpine

A low stone wall makes a superb rock garden where alpine plants add new colours and textures to the stone and link the patio to the garden beautifully.

plants require plenty of light and sun but prefer rocky, well-drained conditions with little soil as in nature. Stunted and refined by centuries of harsh conditions, they have a delicacy and beauty that is almost unreal and collecting plants can become addictive. You should select a sunny spot that is naturally well draining, preferably on a natural slope as this will look most in keeping with the rest of your scheme. If the soil is a little heavy, excavate about 3ft × 3ft (1sq m) and fill with rubble or broken bricks. Alpine plants either love or hate lime so the soil should reflect which group you will be choosing to grow.

The rocks look best if they are local (and will be cheaper to transport); your telephone directory will provide details of local quarries. Positioning your rocks and boulders successfully will be largely a matter of trial and error, so be prepared for some hard work and aching arms before you get it right. It helps to study the formation of rocky outcrops in the wild and to check that you have the grain of the rock running in the correct direction. The stones must be

large enough, too. Small pieces look insubstantial and will not retain sufficient moisture for the plant roots. A plank will prevent your wheelbarrow damaging the rest of the garden but a heavy-duty garden truck is a better option all round.

The actual shape of the feature also requires close attention: it usually describes a kind of arc or horseshoe with the rocks placed with the side of the largest area laid horizontally. The rocks should be placed so that they slope slightly backwards. The next layer of stone is staggered slightly for the most realistic effect. The soil must be well compacted between the rocks to prevent it getting washed away until the plants' roots have established themselves. The rock garden will look a little sparse until some of the cushion and carpet-forming species such as Alyssum and Sedum have had a chance to establish themselves and soften some of the rocky outlines. To give height and weight to the feature, you can add dwarf evergreen conifers which are useful for year-round interest as a great many alpine plants are spring flowering.

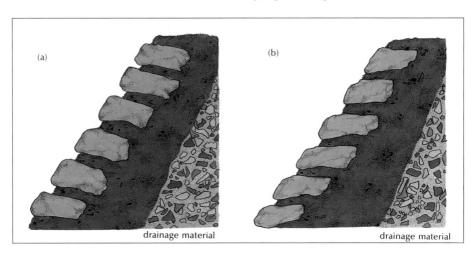

(a)

(b)

drainage material

drainage material

Constructing a rock garden.
(a) Rocks must slope backwards to retain soil and prevent excess water being trapped.
(b) With rocks sloping forwards, soil is easily washed out.

Edibles in the Garden

Eating your own fruit and vegetables is an appealing idea but the traditional vegetable plot doesn't always fit well into the garden plan especially if the site is a small one. You might try screening it from the rest of the garden with trellis or a row of elegant espalier trees, but you must make sure that your screen does not overshadow the area too much. It might be easier and more successful to exploit edible plants' decorative qualities as well as their practical ones and integrate them with the rest of the garden; a useful side benefit to this approach is that you will probably have less trouble with pests and diseases. Just think

Flowering cherries (*Prunus*) are planted primarily as a focal point in small gardens for their wonderful spring blossom and autumn foliage colour. The leaves are an attractive oval shape and the flowers might be single or double blooms. Deciduous types should be given a sunny site and will thrive in most types of soil unless it is poorly drained. Trees can be propagated through softwood cuttings in summer. Some of the Japanese hybrids have very brightly coloured blossom bordering on the lurid so care must be taken when choosing the right position so that it doesn't clash with other nearby flowers and features; a sombre background of evergreens is preferable. There are evergreen *Prunus* and also shrubby forms which can feature interesting bark and autumn fruits as well as spring blossom and foliage colour.

You will often find Sea Holly (*Eryngium*) in the wild, stoutly defying the sea breezes along coastal cliff tops; but it is also valued as an attractive and unusual garden plant, particularly the fully hardy *E. giganteum* whose large thistle-like flowers have such a beautiful metallic-blue colour against the green leaves. The spiky silver bracts give it an other-worldly appearance especially since the plant flowers at the end of summer when many other plants are dying back. Clump-forming *E. giganteum* is a biennial which dies after flowering and reaches a height of around 3–4ft (1–1.2m). Perennial *E. violetta* has an upright habit and a height of 30in (75cm), the thistle flowers a deeper, darker colour. The stems used to be candied as a sweetmeat.

how pretty the foliage of carrot and beetroot are; tiny cherry tomatoes can be grown in hanging baskets and runner beans with their lovely red or white flowers grown as an attractive annual climber up a net or wigwam of poles. Ornamental cabbages like giant colourful roses have already become popular in the flower border; add miniature cauliflowers, sweet pepper plants or those dwarf varieties of peas that need no stick supports.

Edible fruits can be fitted into your general

box

rosemary

lavender

Knot gardens were originally very large and the intertwined geometric shapes might be filled with clipped herbs, box or coloured stones. A scaled-down version can look very effective in today's small urban garden. They are quite time consuming to maintain, but you could enclose the planting beds with brick or stone instead of dwarf edging and fill the spaces with herbs or modern bedding plants.

scheme, too. If you don't think you have room for fruit trees, they can be grown in cordons or espaliers, taking up very little room and providing a good-looking feature into the bargain. The supporting structure might be free-standing or the trees could be grown against a wall or fence. Some trees could be grown in containers on the patio but they will not yield much fruit. Grapevines grow surprisingly well and, being prolific climbers, can be trained in all manner of ways; grow them in the greenhouse or conservatory if you want a good crop. Otherwise use a framework of wires along the south side of the house or any other suitable building. Strawberries can be grown very successfully in containers, and the best space-saving idea is one of those tall strawberry pots which has pockets at regular intervals into which the plants are inserted. You can make one yourself from an old barrel, but generally they are made from plastic or terracotta. In fruit or flower,

they make a charming feature as well as a useful source of many pounds of fruit.

Herbs are another edible plant that have a highly decorative nature. They are adaptable, too, looking good in bed or border, or in containers on the patio. Grow them as a single specimen or in groups of complementary shapes and colours. Herbs are grown as much for their foliage shapes and shades as for their flowers which tend to be small and subtle pinks and mauves. Because they do look good together, they are excellent subjects for design and you will find many ideas for complete herb gardens as well as hedges, herb lawns and seats. A complete garden might take the shape of an informal grouping, close to the kitchen door for easy cropping and a magnet for bees and butterflies. More formal designs are equally popular, the herbs arranged in squares or circles, or in elaborate knot designs in imitation of the traditional Elizabethan gardens.

7 • SEASONAL GUIDE

Spring

● Sow your half-hardy annuals in a greenhouse or coldframe; when the ground is warm enough, sow hardy annuals outside. Later, tender annuals can be sown. Sow under glass any vegetables you have chosen to grow such as cucumbers, lettuce, aubergines, peppers and tomatoes. Keep the seedlings free from weeds and thin when they get too thick. Plant out when the weather is warm enough.
● Alpines can be planted now in your sink or rock garden. Give it a check over, looking for pest infestation and firming in any plants that have been loosened by frost. Start watering regularly if the soil is dry. Trim plants such as aubretia and alyssum after flowering.
● New roses should be planted at the beginning of spring to give them a chance to become established. Prune any established roses and spray before the pests get a hold. Plant under pot-grown standards with attractive carpeting plants to keep weeds down.
● Plant strawberries in strawberry barrels, growbags and tubs.
● Remove spring-flowering bulbs from containers as they start to fade, and replant in the garden. Plant summer-flowering bulbs – in spare pots as well as the garden to liven up your patio containers.
● Plant new evergreens. Prune shrubs where necessary.
● Trim wall-grown ivies.
● As soon as you notice increased activity among pond fish, start feeding. Try a small amount at first, then gradually increase until you find the maximum they will accept.
● If the pond has become clogged, now is the time to change the water. You must first fish out any dead or decaying matter, then pump or empty out by bucket around one third of the water. Take it from the top of the pond so that you do not disturb its biological balance too much. Replace slowly (no

Iris look wonderful wherever they are grown in the garden with their sharp sword-like leaves and elegant large-lipped blooms making an effective contrast to most other plants and complementing similarly spiked rushes and grasses. There are a great many species and cultivars suited to different sites around the garden: you can grow them in beds and borders, in woodland settings, in the rock garden, in bog gardens and beside pools. Different types flower at different times of the year, too, starting in the early spring with the dwarf bulbous irises, so you could plan a continuous display of blooms within the garden virtually right through the year. The Stinking Iris (*I. foetidissima*), generally a pond plant, has bright red fruits through winter, too. Flowers can range from pink, blue and purple to white and yellow.

more than a trickle), preferably with rainwater.
● Pond heaters may be removed when there is no longer any risk of frost.
● Feed lawns with a proprietary fertilizer.

Summer

● Thin flower seedlings and plant out as required. Keep a bed of spares in the garden to fill gaps in beds and containers as required through the season. Deadhead flowers regularly to keep plants blooming, but when finished, remove and replace immediately. Early tomatoes will need staking. Remove extra shoots and keep well watered and fed. As they fruit, crop while they are still young and small.

● Continue to trim and deadhead alpines as required and water sink and rock gardens carefully. Keep free from weeds and look out for slugs. You can propagate from cuttings if you need new plants.

● Keep an eye open for any signs of disease on roses and treat immediately. Deadhead daily and remove suckers. Tie up climbers and ramblers as they make new growth. If you are planning a new sink or rock garden now would be a good time to make it.

● Remove unwanted strawberry runners and use to propagate new plants if you require more. When the crop is over, clear away immediately.

● Lift tulips in pots as soon as they have finished flowering and heel them into the garden. Plant autumn-flowering bulbs in the garden and in spare patio containers for something of interest next season.

● Deadhead azaleas and rhododendrons and trim winter-flowering heathers. Prune

This town garden rockery has something of interest in every season. In spring the freshness of the gold and silver variegated foliage plants which form the backbone of this perpetual display perfectly complement the brightness of spring bulbs.

shrubs as required and clip hedges. Prune wisteria. Water container-planted shrubs and trees diligently.

● Plant new pond varieties in early summer and prune existing plants before they take over. Lift, trim and replant. Make sure there is no risk of frost when planting out water lilies and other aquatic plants.

● Keep an eye open for fish eggs in the pond and transfer them to an aquarium or a nursery pond.

● Water lilies may need thinning out later in the season.

● Remove blanket weed from ponds before it chokes the surface.

● Re-seed or turf lawn repairs as required.

Autumn

● Clear away annual plants as they finish flowering. Continue to sow lettuce and radish in the kitchen garden having cleared away tomatoes, peppers, etc. as they finish. Lift and pot a selection of herbs for overwintering indoors. Fill any gaps in raised beds and containers with ivies, winter pansies and other suitable plants for providing extra interest through winter.

● Plant any small bulbs in the alpine garden. Renew chippings and continue to watch out for slug and snail damage. Generally tidy up. Plants susceptible to damp may need covering with glass or plastic.

● Cut back unwanted new growth or shrub roses. Finish pruning climbers and ramblers.

● Keep paths and the patio clear of dead leaves.

● Order and plant bulbs for spring. Plant early bulbs in special pots and containers for forcing for Christmas.

● Tie up any new growth on climbing plants. Now is a good time to plant new trees and shrubs providing the soil is not frozen.

● Clean up pots, scrubbing where necessary and remove any dead material from the patio area.
● Net ponds to keep free from dead leaves and remove any dead or decaying plants from in and around the water.
● Tender aquatics will need transferring to a tank in a warm greenhouse.
● Wrap *Gunnera manicata* in its own foliage as it dies back to protect it until spring.
● A pond heater will keep the water from freezing over the coming nights. Otherwise, float a plastic ball on the surface to prevent the water freezing completely and damaging the liner.
● If your pond does not have an overflow system, remove about one third of the water and replace in spring.
● Lawns should be scarified with a lawn rake and aerated by puncturing with a fork.

Winter

● Dispose of any growbags and generally tidy up the patio area.
● Make necessary repairs to patio structures and re-stain or varnish timbers where required. Clean paving and disinfect, scrub timber decking free from moss with a stiff wire brush and apply a new coat of preservative if softwoods have been used.
● Make necessary repairs to patio furniture and put into store. Furniture that stays out all winter may require a new coat of paint or preservative before the weather deteriorates.
● Mulching the top of shrub and tree containers will keep them free from weeds and conserve soil warmth.
● Browse through the seed catalogues and pick your colour schemes for next year.
● Cut back clematis and prune other shrubs which carry their flowers on the young wood. When the blooms of winter-flowering jasmine have finished, the

A plant that puts on a brave display in the winter months as well as looking good the rest of the year offers excellent value for smaller gardens. Dogwoods (*Cornus*) need only a well-drained soil and plenty of sunshine to star and one of the best is the red-barked dogwood *C. alba* 'Sibirica' which grows quickly into a hardy shrub with spreading stems. In spring it produces attractive star-shaped white flowers against the dark green leaves, which ripen to oval white fruits with a blue tinge. By autumn the leaves will have turned a reddish-orange hue and through the winter the young stems are a brilliant red colour which make a marvellous display against more sombre plants.

flowering stems should be cut back almost to the old wood. Remove a few of the older stems at the base.
● Plan any major changes to your garden while the majority of plants are dormant. Work can be carried out providing the ground is not frozen or waterlogged.
● Beds will still need to be tidied and occasional weeds dealt with. Mow the lawn occasionally providing the weather is fine and dry and with the mower on its highest setting.
● Should a pond freeze over completely, melt a hole by pouring over hot water to allow gases to escape. Never try to smash your way through, for if you have fish in the pool it will stun them.

GLOSSARY

Acid Having a pH below 7.
Aggregate Stony parts mixed with cement, sand and water to make concrete.
Alkaline Having a pH above 7.
Annual Plant that completes its life-cycle within one growing season.

Basket weave Arrangement of bricks, timber, threads, etc. to resemble the woven pattern of a basket.
Bedding plants Plant, usually an annual, grown *en masse* to create a seasonal effect.
Biennial Plant that produces only stems, roots and leaves in its first season, then flowers and dies in the second.
Bog Area of permanently damp but not waterlogged soil.
Bond Arrangement of bricks.
Butyl Type of rubber often used as a pool-lining material.

Compost Potting mixture either made from peat or coconut fibre known as soil-less compost; or from sterilized soil, known as loam compost.
Container plant Plant which has been grown and sold in a pot or other container. It can be planted at almost any time of year because root disturbance is minimal.
Cordon Plant, usually a fruit tree, restricted to a main stem with a few side stems and trained on wires.
Countersink Sinking the head of a bolt or screw below the surface of the timber.
Course Continuous, usually horizontal layer of building material such as bricks.
Cultivar Variety of a natural plant species that is maintained through cultivation.

Deadheading Removing dead or dying blooms.
Deciduous Plants that lose their foliage annually.
Decking Continuous timbered surface raised off the ground.
Dormant When a plant temporarily stops growing, usually in winter.

Dowel Plug or peg used to join two pieces of timber.

Evergreen Plants which retain their foliage throughout the year.

Fertilizer Chemical that provides plant food.
Focal point Centre of attention; feature which commands most attention.
Fungicide Chemical used to control fungal diseases.

Gazebo Type of open summerhouse or pavilion.
Geometric Composed of simple forms such as circles, rectangles, triangles, etc.
Genus Botanic category denoting a family of related plant species.

Half-hardy Plant usually killed by frost.
Hardcore Broken brick, stones and other rubble used as the foundation before laying concrete, etc.
Hardwood Mature wood taken as a cutting at the end of the growing season.
Hardy Plant tolerant of low temperatures.
Herbaceous plants Non-woody or soft-stemmed plants, usually border perennials.
Herringbone Pattern used in brickwork and textiles where two or more rows of short parallel strokes slant in alternate directions to create a series of parallel zigzags.
Hybrid Plant resulting from a cross between two genetically unlike individuals.

Insecticide Chemical which kills insects.

Landscaping Laying out a garden, usually in imitation of natural features.
Loam Good fertile soil.

Microclimate Atmospheric conditions relating to a small group.
Mortar Mixture of cement or lime or both with sand to create a bond between brick or stones.

Mulch Material spread on the surface of the soil around a plant to conserve moisture and suppress weeds.
Mural Large painting or picture on a wall.

Orientation Position in relation to the points of a compass: i.e. north, south, east, west.

Panicle Flower spike.
Peat Partially decomposed plant material traditionally used to improve soil but recently replaced by other materials such as coconut fibre due to the decline in boglands.
Perennials Long-lived plants which appear each year.
Pergola Horizontal trellis or framework sometimes creating a walkway and designed as a support for climbing plants.
Porous Able to absorb water.
Pot-bound Stage when the plant roots are cramped in the container.
Potting-on Placing plant in a new, larger pot when it outgrows its old one.
Propagate To reproduce plant by seeds, cuttings, etc.
Prostrate Creeping along the ground.

Rustic Simple, country style.

Semi-ripe Half-ripened wood taken as a cutting during the growing season.
Softwood Young growth which is taken for cuttings at the beginning of the growing season.
Species Subdivisions of a genus.
Spirit Level Tool for checking that a vertical or horizontal surface is completely level.
Subsoil Layer of soil beneath the surface soil and above the bedrock.
Symmetrical Having two sides perfectly balanced.
Systemic Pesticide or fungicide which spreads through all parts of the plant without damaging it.

Tubs of evergreens and/or seasonal plants can add a little seasonal flair on the patio or in the garden at any time. These bright yellow calceolaria against a background of variegated ivy are an unmistakable eye-catcher.

Tender Plant which requires protection from low temperatures.
Terracotta Hard, unglazed russet-red earthenware.
Topiary Trimming or training trees and shrubs into ornamental shapes.
Topsoil Fertile soil on top of the ground.
Transpire To lose water.
Trellis Structure of latticework useful for climbing plants.
Trompe l'oeil Painting or decoration giving the impression of reality.

Variegated Leaves marked in a secondary colour.
Versailles planter Style of plant container featuring wood or fibreglass panels raised on four feet and sometimes with finial decorations.

Weeping Plant whose branches have been trained or which grow naturally in a hanging, pendant way.

INDEX